CW00920664

Boris Johnson's Funniest Quotes

By Sebastian Windsor

SebastianWindsor

First published 2024

CONTENTS

INTRODUCTION

Boris Johnson speaks like no other politician.

He jokes, jibes and jousts with his opponents.

He entertains supporters with mocking one-liners, wise-cracking puns and vivid metaphors.

Sebastian Windsor, author of the in-depth analysis of Boris's rhetoric: ***Boris Banter – The Eccentric Oratory of Boris Johnson*** has now distilled more than 200 of the funniest Boris quips here in this concise book: ***The Little Gift Book of Boris Johnson's Funniest Quotes***.

Boris on bendy buses:

"We've begun the elimination of the bendy bus. It won't be long before the last pair of breeding bendy buses is driven from our streets."

Boris on his privileged upbringing:

"At Eton I was the beneficiary of a scholarship endowed by Henry VI. If that isn't state education, I don't know what is."

Boris on free trade:

"Only the free market could produce something as ingenious as an ice cream Snickers bar."

Attacking Labour leader Keir Starmer:

"Captain Hindsight is rising rapidly up the ranks and has become General Indecision. That is what is happening, I am afraid, to the right honourable and learned gentleman. He dithers. We get on with the job."

Boris on messing up:

Boris: *"My strategy is to litter my career with so many decoy mistakes nobody knows which one to attack."*

On upsetting people:

"It's absolutely wonderful to be here in Manchester – one of the few great British cities I have yet to insult."

Boris on hotels:

"If you think about the image of British versus

American hoteliers: I think we may have Fawlty Towers but then they have Psycho. On the whole I think I'd rather be shown to my room by Basil Fawlty than Norman Bates."

Boris citing Kermit the frog:

"When Kermit the frog sang It's Not Easy Being Green I want you to know he was wrong. And he was also unnecessarily rude to Miss Piggy."

Attacking the SNP:

"We will take back control of our fisheries and the extraordinary marine wealth of Scotland. And it's one of the many bizarre features of the SNP that in spite of being called names like Salmond and Sturgeon they are committed to handing back control of those fish to the EU. We want to turbo-charge the Scottish fishing sector: they would allow Brussels to charge for our turbot."

On emperors:

"I am proud to say today that one in seven of the world's Kings, Queens, Presidents, Prime Ministers were educated in this country including the Japanese Emperor. We have a total global monopoly on the higher education of emperors. Thank you – it's true."

On architecture:

"Only in London could they decide to ensconce the mayor in a building which is a cross between a pile of collapsing pancakes and Darth Vader's helmet."

Enjoy *The Little Gift Book of Boris Johnson's Funniest Quotes.*

BORIS AND HIS LIFE

FAMILY

"My mother is a painter and I've always wanted to paint very badly myself. And indeed do - paint very badly."

Speaking at the American Enterprise Institute annual dinner, in 2018.

"It was only 85 years ago that my grandfather was flying Wellington bombers with equipment so primitive that you really have to marvel at the bravery of the men and women who were involved in that war. In fact he used up quite a few Wellington bombers. He crashed twice - the second time into a church. I am afraid he was always prone to religious doubts."

Speech as Prime Minister opening the 2022 Farnborough Air Show. Boris's grandfather was Wilfred 'Johnny' Johnson. A Wellington Mk XIV he was piloting during the Second World War, in 1944, crashed after an engine failed in an incident that claimed the lives of the plane's navigator and air gunner at the Chivenor Royal Air Force Station. Boris's grandfather was awarded the Distinguished Flying Cross for his actions that prevented further casualties. A memorial service to remember those who died at Chivenor during the war was held at what is now Royal Marines Barracks Chivenor, in 2019, during which Boris's father Stanley Johnson said: "The accident was my first childhood memory on the eve of my fourth birthday. My mother woke me up to see the conflagration little knowing that my father was the pilot of the aircraft." Wilfred Johnson was himself seriously injured in the crash, sustaining severe burns and a broken leg.

CHILDHOOD

*"We didn't have car seats when I was a nipper.
We just bounced around in the back of the car like
peas in a rattle, landing on our heads.   It never
did us any harm."*

Speaking at University of Surrey
Students' Union, 2007.

ETON SCHOOL

"At Eton I was the beneficiary of a scholarship endowed by Henry VI. If that isn't state education, I don't know what is."

Speaking to journalist Steve Richards, for School Days, a Teachers TV /Department of Education production, 2006.

BEHAVIOUR AND CHARACTER

"What you've got to bear in mind is that behind the carefully cultivated veneer of a blithering idiot is that there is a blithering idiot a lot of the time."

Speaking to journalist Steve Richards, in 2006, for School Days, a Teachers TV /Department of Education production about his bumbling persona on the topical BBC TV news quiz Have I Got News For You.

"As a general tactic in life it is often useful to give the slight impression that you are deliberately pretending not to know what is going on. Because the reality may be that you don't know what is going on but people won't be able to tell the difference."

Speaking on the BBC documentary: Boris Johnson, The Irresistible Rise - first broadcast in 2013.

OXFORD UNIVERSITY

Boris studied Classics at Oxford and became a prominent figure in the Oxford Union debating society. He was elected president of the union – at the second attempt.

"Who is it that we can thank for the economically invaluable fact that English is the international language of business, of fashion, of movies and air traffic control? Who do we have to thank for

that? It was that 14th century Balliol man John Wycliffe who had the brilliant idea of writing the bible in a language that people could actually read. Or rather, actually, getting his students to do it for him: a practice not unknown to dons in Balliol today."

Speaking at the 750th anniversary celebrations of Balliol College, Oxford, while Mayor of London, 2013. Boris studied at Balliol from 1983 to 1987. Howard

Marks studied at Balliol in the 1960s. The following two quotes are from the same speech.

"That was an epoch when the life expectancy at birth was only thirty-one-and-a-half; when the tiny handful of Oxford proto-undergraduates were characterised by ignorance, vile religious bigotry, striking dermatological complaints and – most tragic of all – an inability to speak English. In other words they spoke much like Trinity **[College]** *today."*

"Except among consenting adults and unless administered with the right degree of love, tact and anatomical accuracy – as will no doubt take place tonight in dimly lit bedrooms across Oxford and the Home Counties at the conclusion of this riotous dinner – we liberal-minded Balliol men and women do not normally approve of flagellation. We deplore it, we're opposed to it, we fought against it: I'm sure that Balliol men and women made sure that it wasn't part of the punitive system of our country. And 750 years later we grieve anew for the smarting rear end of our great co-founder John de Balliol. We regard it as an outrage that he should have been whipped in broad daylight on the steps of Durham Cathedral for what today would be regarded as the minor transgression of kidnapping and teasing a bishop."

APPEARING ON HAVE I GOT NEWS FOR YOU

Ian Hislop: *"Boris was on tape talking to Darius Guppy."*

Boris: *"A great chap."*

Ian Hislop: *"A great chap, despite being a convicted fraudster."*

Boris: *"Convicted fraudster. Went very sadly wrong. Major goof."*

Ian Hislop: *"And one of the ways he went wrong is ringing you up on tape and suggesting that you help him beat up a journalist who was looking into him."*

Boris: *"That did come up. I won't deny that did come up. I'm not ashamed of it."*

Angus Deayton, presenter: *"What are you not ashamed of, Boris?"*

Boris: *"Whatever there is not to be ashamed of."*

Speaking on Have I Got News For You, 1998, when confronted by Ian Hislop about his conversation with Darius Guppy where Guppy asked for details of a journalist he wanted to intimidate.

No assault took place. But the conversation, from 1990, was recorded.

The journalist was Stuart Collier of the News of the World. Speaking to The Guardian in 2019, Collier, who left the NoW in the late 1990s, said: "This wasn't just a joking matter. He was going to help Guppy all he could." Guppy was jailed for five years in 1993 after being convicted of an insurance fraud based on a fake robbery of jewellery.

Writing in The Spectator in March 2013, Guppy defended Boris. He said: "As we all know, Mr Johnson never provided me with any address. It is perfectly clear from the tape recording in question that he was simply placating a friend whom he considered to be letting off steam."

BEING MAYOR OF LONDON

Boris defeated Ken Livingstone to become mayor in 2008. It gave him a chance to govern one of the world's great cities. He stood up at events across the city, the UK and worldwide to celebrate London, its people and achievements. He served a second four-year term after defeating Livingstone again in 2012.

"There is a quite dizzying amount of executive authority that you wield as Mayor of London. Probably quite terrifying for some of the people who know me."

Speaking on BBC Hard Talk, 2009.

CONSERVATIVE PARTY LEADER AND PRIME MINISTER

Boris succeeded Theresa May to become Tory leader and Prime Minister in July 2019. She had struggled to cope with the divisions in Parliament following the Brexit vote of 2016. When Boris could not get support for his plans in the House of Commons he called a general election in December 2019 that gave him an 80-seat majority and the highest share of the popular vote since Margaret Thatcher won the 1979 election. His reign lasted until September 2022.

Interviewer: *"What's the most surprising thing*

you've found about being PM?"

Boris: *"I was pretty incredulous the other day when I found I that I couldn't actually get a Thai curry to deliver to Number 10 because of the security problems, the security was too tight."*

Speaking in a Conservative Party election video, 2019

"I want to begin by thanking my opponent, Jeremy [Jeremy Hunt]. By common consent an absolutely formidable campaigner and a great leader and a great politician. Jeremy, in the course of 20 hustings-style events - about 7,000 miles that we did criss-crossing the country - you've been friendly, you've been good natured. You've been a font of excellent ideas, all of which I propose to steal forthwith."

Victory speech at event to announce next leader of Conservative Party (and Prime Minister) after he defeated Jeremy Hunt in leadership election, 2019.

23

BEING OVERWEIGHT

"You know - looking around at this illustrious audience here at the IOD [Institute of Directors] *I observe one thing, certainly about myself. We British are not hobbits. We are not getting conspicuously smaller. In fact, we are getting if anything fatter and fatter. I'm afraid we are. I can barely do up my jacket."*

Speaking as Mayor of London at the 2009 Institute of Directors Annual Convention at the Royal Albert Hall.

EXERCISE

"During my two years as Foreign Secretary I visited more African nations than any other senior British politician in living memory: Ghana, the Gambia, Libya, Liberia, Uganda, Nigeria, Côte D'Ivoire, Somalia, Kenya, Egypt, Ethiopia - where in a fit of brilliance our excellent ambassador decided that I should challenge Haile Gebrselassie to a running race in Addis Ababa at an altitude of 2,355 metres, and in fierce sunshine, over a distance of about a mile. And I had to pretend to have a heart attack in order to get him to slow down. And what everybody said was that it was a very convincing impersonation of a man having a heart attack."

Speech as Prime Minister at UK-Africa Investment Summit, 2020.

Long distance runner Haile Gebrselassie won two 10,000-metre gold medals, at the 1996 and 2000 Olympic Games - in Atlanta and Sydney.

BEING A PUBLIC FIGURE

Interviewer Arthur C Brooks: *"Tell me the biggest mistake you've made in your public career and what you've learned from it."*

Boris: *"My strategy is to litter my career with so many decoy mistakes nobody knows which one to attack."*

Speaking at the American Enterprise Institute annual dinner, 2018.

On causing offence

"It's absolutely wonderful to be here in Manchester – one of the few great British cities I have yet to insult."

Speaking at Conservative Party
Conference, Manchester, 2009.

Beth Rigby of Sky News: *"Mr Johnson, you brandish your Brexit credentials but many of your colleagues worry about your character."*

Boris: *"My parrot?"*

Beth Rigby: *"Your character."*

LANGUAGE

Boris uses a huge toolbox of linguistic utensils to bring colour to his public speaking. Whether he is on the stump campaigning, answering questions in a television studio or making a prepared speech to a business dinner he invariably inserts metaphors, hyperbolic claims, quirky vocabulary, jokes and slang. These are often interspersed with a range of allusions: to the bible, classical civilisation, science, historical figures and modern popular culture. He might quote a line from Morecambe and Wise in one sentence before referencing Pericles of Athens in the next.

RHYME

"I know there has been a certain raucous squawkus from the anti-AUKUS caucus."

Speaking in 2021 at the Conservative party conference, Manchester.

Squawk has the meaning of a bird, or person, making a loud noise or screech. AUKUS is a security collaboration agreement between Australia, the UK and USA aimed at securing what the countries call a secure and stable Indo-Pacific region. AUKUS has two main areas of work, defined as "pillars". The first is for Australia to get hold of nuclear-powered attack submarines and for these to be supported by others from the UK and USA. The second pillar sees the three nations working together on electronic warfare, quantum technologies, AI, cyber warfare and hypersonic and counter hypersonic activity. AUKUS was formed in September 2021 and was accompanied by a decision by the Australians to cancel an order for 12 French submarines in favour of examples from the UK and USA. The move caused upset in French governmental circles with Foreign Minister Jean-Yves Le Drian calling it a

"stab in the back."

"We are getting on with the job. They jabber, we jab. They dither, we deliver. They vacillate and we vaccinate."

Speaking in House of Commons, PM's questions, 2021.

UNUSUAL VOCABULARY

"Are you saying they are abdicating their duty to scrutinise me? Are you saying they haven't the guts to put questions to me? Great supine protoplasmic invertebrate jellies!"

Speaking to members of the London Assembly after they moved to a vote rather than question him as mayor about council tax cuts, 2013.

Supine means to fail to act because of moral weakness. A protoplasm is part of a cell surrounded by a plasma membrane. Invertebrates are cold blooded animals without a backbone. Jellies are wobbly desserts.

PUNS

"I speak feelingly because I was once a director myself of a tile company, which lasted all of about 24 hours. You could say I spent a night on the tiles."

Speaking as Mayor of London at the 2013 Institute of Directors Annual Convention.

Boris: *"We need new fencing. We need to remove some weeds. We need new decking apparently. Do we need decking?"*

Crowd: *"Yes!"*

Boris: *"Some people think I need decking. There are plenty of people who think I need decking."*

Speaking as Mayor of London on a visit to Harrow Cricket Club where he was seeing how they were refurbishing the club.

"Hopefully, as we said at our bilateral, when it comes to chilled meats the wurst is behind us."

> Speaking as UK Prime Minister at a press conference alongside German chancellor Angela Merkel about border trade restrictions, 2021.
>
> Wurst, in German, is sausage.

"Lagos is the London of Africa but it's also the Dublin of Africa. Because they brew Guinness. And because it's doublin' every decade. [Pause] That joke needs work."

> Speaking to Rehumanising Conference, Lagos, Nigeria, 2023.

"He makes a contrast between this Government and his own proposals. The contrast could not be clearer: we think that the friends of this country are to be found in Paris, in Berlin and in the White House, and he thinks that they are in the Kremlin, in Tehran and - he does - and in Caracas.
And I think he is c-ra-ckers."

SebastianWindsor

Speaking in House of Commons,
PM's Questions, referencing then
Labour leader Jeremy Corbyn,

2019.

BIBLICAL ALLUSION

"In rowing, alone, I think they have contributed the greatest aquatic triumph this country has seen since Trafalgar. And, when you look at their achievement, I think you will agree we are not worthy to loose the latchet of their shoes and you will ask: "How can I accept this award tonight?"

"It is because I am a politician.

"And because: in a world notoriously short of credit I'm determined to hoover it up while it's going. And on the very good principle that I would almost certainly have been unjustly blamed had things have gone wrong I have no hesitation or compunction in accepting this fantastic award tonight, ladies and gentlemen, on the strict understanding that it is not a recognition for me but a recognition of everybody who works for London, the greatest city on Earth."

Speaking to accept an award at the GQ Men of the Year Awards, after the success of the London Olympics, 2012.

The biblical allusion made here by Boris is from the New Testament - Luke 3:16. The quote is spoken by John the Baptist to describe the coming of Christ.

The text says: "And he said unto them,

"Exact no more than that which is appointed you.

"And the soldiers likewise demanded of him, saying,

"And what shall we do?

"And he said unto them,

"Do violence to no man, neither accuse any falsely; and be content with your wages.

"And as the people were in expectation, and all men mused in their hearts of John, whether he were the Christ, or not;

"John answered, saying unto them all,

"I indeed baptize you with water;

"But one mightier than I cometh, the latchet of whose shoes I am not worthy to unloose:

"He shall baptize you with the Holy Ghost and with fire:

"Whose fan is in his hand,

"And he will thoroughly purge his floor,

"And will gather the wheat into his garner; but the chaff he will burn with fire unquenchable.

"And many other things in his exhortation preached he unto the people."

METAPHOR

Metaphor is one of Boris's signature linguistic devices. He uses it to celebrate. He uses it to denigrate and poke fun. A favourite food based metaphor is to call a political opponent's observations a "minestrone of nonsense". He cheerfully compared David Cameron and members of his cabinet to a broom, dustpan, jay cloth and sponge – implying that together they were cleaning up after the previous Labour administration. His speeches and replies to questions are seasoned with metaphors and he clearly enjoys looking for them to express a point, to add colour, to convey images.

"I was pleased to see that you've called me a blond haired mop. If I'm a mop, Dave [**David Cameron**], *then you are a broom. A broom that is clearing up the mess left behind by the Labour government. I congratulate you and your colleagues George Osborne, the dustpan; Michael Gove, the jay cloth; William Hague, the*

sponge. It is the historic function of Conservative governments over the last 100 years to be the household implements so effective on the floor of the house to clear things up after the Labour binge has got out of control."

Speaking to Conservative Party
Conference, 2012.

Sir John Hayes, Conservative MP for South Holland and The Deepings: *"In 1801 Horatio Nelson, perhaps our nation's greatest hero, chose not to see advice to retreat. In that spirit, will the Prime Minister turn a blind eye to the antics of the liberal establishment, and turn a deaf ear to the shrill bleats of those who seek to foil Brexit and frustrate the will of the people? For he must know that the loud and clear cry of the working people of this country is as straightforward as this: "Back Brexit and back Boris.""*

Boris: *"I thank my right honourable friend. I will not only try to imitate Horatio Nelson; I will lash myself to the mast, figuratively speaking, like Odysseus and stop my ears to the siren cries of those opposite who would try to frustrate the will of the people and block Brexit. That is what they want to do, but we are not going to let them do it."*

Speaking in House of Commons,
Prime Minister's Update, 2019.

Odysseus was the mythical Greek
king of Ithaca and the hero of
The Odyssey, by Homer. It is
said that he ordered the crew of
his ship to tie him to the mast so
he would not been tempted by
creatures with bird-like bodies
and the heads of women, known
as sirens. Sirens were said to lure
sailors to small rocky islands
where they and their vessels
would founder and perish.

"This [the United Kingdom] *is the great
cultural Moulinex of the world. The cyclotron of
talent."*

Speech as Prime Minister, 2021,
Global Investment Summit,

Science Museum, London.

Moulinex is a French company
long-famous for its range of
food blenders, grinders, pulpers
and squeezers. A cyclotron is a
particle accelerator developed
by American nuclear physicist
Ernest Lawrence, in 1931. It
can produce high energy beams
for experiments in nuclear
physics. Cyclotrons continue
to be used in the present day
for medical applications such
as radiotherapy. A cyclotron is
included in the proton pack used

by the fictional heroes of the 1984 movie Ghostbusters - to catch ghosts.

Caroline Noakes, Conservative MP for Romsey and Southampton North: *"There is a blockage in the system; I urge my right honourable friend to get out his plunger and make sure that the Department for Environment, Food and Rural Affairs, the Ministry of Housing, Communities and Local Government, Natural England and the Environment Agency all work together to protect our waterways, to make sure that housing commitments can be met."*

Boris: *"We will make sure that the ministerial Dyno-Rod is employed to sort out the blockage that my right honourable friend is experiencing."*

Speaking in House of Commons, PM's questions, 2020.

Dyno-Rod is a UK plumbing business most popularly known for unblocking bunged-up drains.

Katherine Fletcher, Conservative MP for South Ribble: *"Can the Prime Minister confirm that while there might be tough days ahead, this Conservative Government are throwing the kitchen sink at fixing it?"*

41

Boris: *"It is not only the kitchen sink, but every part of the kitchen. We are going to build, build, build our way forward. We are going to be supporting the building of 300,000 new homes a year. We are going to do everything we can to ensure that we get jobs, jobs, jobs throughout this country. Whether by installing kitchen sinks or any other part of the house, we will take this country forward."*

Speaking in House of Commons,
PM's questions, 2020.

"At the risk of sounding more North Korean than normal, Saj [Sajid Javid, then Chancellor of the Exchequer] *has passed me some good economic news – employment is up again, unemployment is down again. The economy continues to be robust but we will now take steps to strengthen it further."*

Speaking at first Cabinet meeting
after December election victory,
2019.

Absolute Radio reporter*: "What's been your biggest headache so far?"*

Boris: *"It moves around: it's a lumpy mattress, isn't it? You press down one bit and another bit pops up. You press down that, another bit pops up. You can really never let up."*

Speaking to Absolute Radio at the hanging of the Olympic rings from Tower Bridge, London, one month before the opening of the 2012 Olympic Games.

"Out of that minestrone of nonsense has floated a crouton of fact - is that he is going to vote against the measures tonight. They are going to vote against plans to fix the backlogs and to fix social care. Vote Labour, Mr Speaker, wait longer."

Speaking in House of Commons, PM's questions, 2021.

In response to Labour leader Keir Starmer.

"Everybody's got to take some pain. We've got a huge deficit in this country. The cost of servicing that debt is colossal. People are going to have to retrench in the public sector. The point I've been making to Government is not to forget that here in London we've already been making those cuts in the last two years. We've greatly reduced the number of employees in Transport for London, down by eight per cent; the LDA – London Development Agency, virtually halved. I could take you downstairs: there's a sort of Mary Celeste floor here in City Hall because so many

people have gone off and done other things."

Speaking as Mayor of London, asked about jobs cuts after the financial crisis, interviewed by Mumsnet, 2010.

The Mary Celeste was a merchant ship that was found adrift with none of its crew present in waters near The Azores, in the Atlantic Ocean, in 1872. The ship's lifeboat was missing but it was still seaworthy and the crew had left behind a cargo of alcohol and their personal possessions. A number of explanations were speculated on at a subsequent inquiry including piracy or mutiny but no cause was established.

Telegraph reporter: *"If the EU were an animal what would it be?"*

Boris: *"The EU is an animal that has been designed by a committee. The EU is one of those heraldic, mythical hippogriffs or beast. Or chimeras: it is a chimera. It has – I think somebody once said the EU...is...er, you know, um, in some way - in heaven...what is it the thing where all the cooks are British? Anyway, I can't remember the joke. But anyway: the EU is a – I tell you what the EU is: if the EU* *were an animal, I tell you what it would be, symbolically. The EU would be a lobster. Because the EU, by the very way it works, encourages its participating members to order the lobster at the joint meal because they know that the bill is going to be settled by everybody else: normally by the Germans. So that's what the EU would be, it would be a gigantic lobster with a butter sauce or something like that."*

Speaking about his time as Brussels correspondent for The Daily Telegraph, 2014.

Hippogriffs are creatures of legend with the front half of an eagle and the rear of a horse.

"In our government we've got a wonderful, magnificent example of a waltz – a great coalition waltz between Nick Clegg and David Cameron, followed by William Hague break-dancing down Whitehall."

Speaking as Mayor of London at Big Dance, London, 2010.

"I think of the pogonologically challenged Labour party where they literally want to abolish our armed services. And to keep our nuclear submarines as a kind of demented job creation

programme, sending them to sea without any nukes aboard so the whole nation is turned into a kind of glorified military capon. Firing blanks."

Speaking at Conservative Party Conference, Manchester, 2016.

Pogonology is the study of beards. Boris references the bearded nature of north London Labour members from time to time. A capon is a male chicken – cockerel – that has been castrated to

improve its flavour for eating.

"I see the honourable and learned gentleman rise from his seat like a rocketing pheasant. Well, like a very slowly rocketing pheasant. I think that I can anticipate what he will say, but I will let him say it."

Speaking in House of Commons, debate on the Police and Justice Bill, 2006. Boris was anticipating a question from Labour MP Robert Marshall-Andrews, MP for Medway.

"On the subject of bouncing around and future careers let me say that I am now like one of those booster rockets that has fulfilled its function and I will now be gently re-entering the atmosphere and splashing down invisibly in some remote and obscure corner of the Pacific."

Final speech as Prime Minister,
Downing Street, 2022.

LONDON

Boris served two terms as Mayor of London between 2008 and 2016. He became the first and only Conservative winner of a mayoral election – his reign being preceded by Ken Livingstone and followed by Sadiq Khan, both Labour. While in office he gave speeches extolling the merits of London as a city of enterprise, commerce, education, research, science and technology. And his time in office coincided with the 2012 London Olympics, which gave his oratory ample opportunity to be unleashed at public celebrations.

QUALITY OF LIFE

"We're improving air quality. Air quality in London now is virtually of Alpine freshness. There was a moment recently when there was a poor air quality day. And the air was worse in Norfolk than it was in London. The day is not far off when the children of Norfolk will be bussed in to London to breathe in deep gulps of Hyde Park air."

Speaking at the Brookings Institution, Washington DC, as Mayor of London at an event to discuss governing growing global cities, 2015.

"One of the reasons, by the way, that we are seeing such a dramatic fall in deaths by fire - do you know this? We have seen huge reductions in deaths by fire in London. And that's because Londoners are no longer accidentally and drunkenly carbonising themselves in late night chip pan fires because the range of late night food is so fantastic and so wonderful. We have, as I never tire of telling you, more Michelin-starred restaurants than Paris itself: a statistic

I haven't bothered to verify recently but I'm sure I'm prepared to do so."

> Speaking as Mayor of London,
> 2015, at the Legatum Institute's
> Vision of Capitalism. The
> Legatum Institute is a think tank
> devoted to the promotion of
> prosperity.

LIFE EXPECTANCY OF LONDONERS

"The average life expectancy according to my brief – unless there's some misprint – the average life expectancy in the Harrow Road is 97.1 years' old. They're living longer than the Japanese, living longer than Caucasian hermits whose diet is entirely yoghurt and apricots and olives and what have you."

Speaking as Mayor of London at the annual London Government Dinner at Mansion House, City of London, 2014.

Monastic hermits are a feature in some of the mountains of the Caucasus region which exists between the Black Sea and Caspian Sea and includes Armenia, Azerbaijan, Georgia and areas of southern Russia. A visitor to Abkhazia, on the eastern Black Sea coast, has reported how hermits live,

51

including details of what they eat. Writing anonymously, for the Othodox Christian website, he said: "The hermits' diet mainly consists of herbs that grow near the cell (burdock and nettle) and vegetables. Some beans and potatoes grow in the garden. To break the fast for the feasts with fish you need to walk down to the river, but the descent is so difficult that the enterprise is not worth the "consolation". Once, the monks planted peach trees. But as soon as they began to bear fruit, a bear came (there are many of them here), broke up the trees and ate all the fruit."

"Average life expectancy for both men and women in London has gone up by about 18 months since 2008. You live longer under the Conservatives, right? That is a gift beyond price. Eighteen more months to dangle the grandchildren and make jam and take up hang gliding and slow-clap politicians and use your freedom pass. Eighteen more months to pose naked for Women's Institute calendars."

Speaking as Mayor of London, at the Legatum Institute's Vision of Capitalism event, 2015. The institute is a think tank devoted to the promotion of prosperity.

"Just since I've been mayor, I am proud to say, life

expectancy has gone up in London by 18 months for women and 19 months for men. Men are catching up obviously. And there are parts of the Harrow Road now where life expectancy at birth is 97. I don't know what monkey glands or royal jelly they apply in the Harrow Road – but you live longer under the Tories, my friends."

Speaking to Conservative party conference, Manchester, 2015.

LONDON VS PARIS

"It was only the other day, ladies and gentlemen, that I had the final confirmation that this is the most attractive and sought-after city in Europe: when I read that not only is former French president Nicolas Sarkozy in search of a London address – as he flees the tyrannous taxation of the socialist government in Paris. But even better – he is bringing his wife, Carla Bruni. And I can imagine that the news has broken like a thunderclap over the grief stricken people of Paris. And they are begging Carla to stay behind. And the partisans of Paris are saying that London is nowhere near stylish or sophisticated enough to receive the chinchilla-clad form of Carla and her Cuban-heeled paramour."

Speaking as Mayor of London at the Chartered Institute of Housing's Presidential Dinner, Natural History Museum, 2013.

Boris was speaking after press reports in the UK that Sarkozy planned to escape France's 75 per cent tax rate for high earners and move with his former fashion model wife Carla Bruni to London. The rumoured move was alleged to have been contained in documents found by investigators looking into fraud allegations against the former French president, who served in the role between 2007 and 2012.

"We certainly have more museums than Paris and more theatres but we're also, I'm absolutely certain of this, a city that exports: tea to China, from Sutton; bikes to Holland, from Chiswick; TV aerials to Korea, from Wandsworth; cake – chocolate cake – in ever growing quantities, from Waltham Forest - to France. And I was delighted to see we export scent, lavender scent: grown, picked, distilled, perfected in the London borough of Croydon. From Croydon to Paris, ladies and gentlemen, it's absolutely true. And that is the city that they will find. I also want them to find a city – and this is the key point – I want them to find a city where the PA who has to deal with Nicolas and the aromatherapist who emery-boards, or whatever aromatherapists do, Carla's nails; the safer neighbourhood officers who will keep their streets amongst the safest in Europe; the teacher who instructs the little Sarkozettes in English; the chauffeur, the waiters: all the Londoners who will benefit one way or another from the arrival of this French cash, I want them all to be able to live within a reasonable distance of their place of work."

Speaking as Mayor of London
at the Chartered Institute of
Housing's Presidential Dinner,
Natural History Museum, 2013.

"I say to our friend, monsieur Hollande, still reeling as he is from the discovery that London is now the fourth biggest French city – I say to monsieur Hollande: "Monsieur le President, never mind. Never mind: if things get too tough for you over there, Monsieur le President, just put on your famous crash helmet, get on your scooter and join the exodus to Londres where you will find - amongst many other wonderful attractions - a civilised and gentle media who would never dream, who would never dream, who would never dream of being so vulgar as to discuss your personal affairs.""

Speaking as Mayor of London at
the annual London Government
Dinner at Mansion House, City of
London, 2014.

President François Hollande of
France was revealed in 2014
to have been having an affair.
The French were said to have
been far more scandalised by
the revelation not that he was
cheating on his partner but
that he made assignations with
his mistress, actor Julie Gayet,
by scooting across Paris on a
125cc Piaggio MP3. Hollande
was pictured riding the scooter
dressed in a smart suit and
wearing a helmet. He and his

partner, Paris Match journalist Valérie Trierweiler, split up following the revelations. Hollande and Gayet married in 2022. The scooter sold for 20,500 Euros at auction in 2024. The Piaggio MP3 is a three-wheeled tilting scooter with two wheels at the front and one at the rear.

LONDON VS GENEVA

"The best advertisement for London is a night out in Geneva."

Speaking to Jeremy Paxman on Newsnight when Mayor of London about public feelings of anger towards bankers after the crash and in the early days of the coalition Conservative / Lib Dem Government.

LONDON VS ANCIENT ATHENS

"Let us continue, for as long as Londoners have legs and as long as Londoners have nerves, to show the rest of Europe that here in this city we keep alive the ancient skill of those soldiers we see on those Athenian friezes. By the way, you can see them on the walls of the Athenaeum, just outside. Keep alive the ancient skill of those soldiers who were trained to be able to board and alight from a moving chariot. And let us defy the health and safety fanatics from Brussels by mounting and dismounting the open platform of those beautiful new Routemasters with the freedom and grace of the hop-on, hop-off Hoplites of Periclean Athens."

Speaking on Athenian
Civilisation as Mayor of London
to the Legatum Institute - a think

tank devoted to the promotion of prosperity, 2014.

The Athenaeum Club in Pall Mall, London, is a gentlemen's club – which since 2002 has also been open to women. It was founded in 1824 and its exterior walls are decorated with a frieze which is a copy of the frieze at the Parthenon in Athens, Greece. The London frieze was made by Scottish Sculptor John Henning and his son, also named John.

Greek city states employed citizen soldiers known as Hoplites. Hoplite is still used as a term for infantry soldiers in modern Greece.

Boris introduced a new Routemaster series of buses in 2012 as Mayor of London, having promised during his first election campaign in 2008 to replace the old Routemaster buses. The vehicles had an open back door that passengers could hop-on to and hop-off from, even between stops when the bus was moving slowly enough. Such buses employed conductors. Boris was keen to promote the rear access platform of the new Routemaster. Boris's successor as London mayor, Sadiq Khan, ended London's purchase of the buses. The new Routemaster buses were later converted to enable entry for passengers through the front doors only, ending boarding via the rear doors.

LONDON VS THE REST OF THE UK

"I want to tackle one of the great myths and one of the most pernicious myths of our time: namely, that London is somehow drifting apart from the rest of the country - as if it were some lunar module about to detach itself while the booster-doodahs slump back to earth."

Speaking at the London School of Economics, on The Future of London Within the UK, 2013.

LONDON AS A GLOBAL CITY

"As Mayor of London I have the government of effectively a city state that is bigger than Austria, bigger than Belgium, bigger than Sweden, bigger than most of the countries in the EU. I mean, I should have a place in the European Council of Ministers."

Speaking in an interview as Mayor of London with Al Jazeera on the programme: Boris Johnson: Towering Over London, 2013.

*"I've just been told today that we are now up to between three hundred and four hundred thousand French ressortissant [**French nationals**] here in London and we are therefore now the fourth biggest French city on earth. We are bigger than Bordeaux, we are bigger than Nantes, we are bigger than Strasbourg itself. Any bigger, my friends, and we will have to worry about the possibility of a German invasion. That*

is a joke! That's a joke, that's a joke. For the benefit of all international diplomats here tonight - that's a joke. Don't panic. As Rutilius Namatianus said of his city, Rome, in 417 AD: "We have taken a city and we have made it the world.""

Speaking as Mayor of London at the annual London Government Dinner at Mansion House, City of London, 2014.

Rutilius Claudius Namaitanus was a Roman poet who wrote in praise of his home city.

"We do have huge numbers of French people – I'm the mayor of the fourth biggest French city on earth. There are approximately 400,000 French men and women in London. That's more than Nantes, it's more than Strasbourg. I'd have to worry about a German invasion if we go on with this kind of level of French – it's a joke by the way. And a joke that I've made before, in case any members of the media think it's worth reporting."

Speaking at the Brookings Institution, Washington DC, as Mayor of London at an event to discuss governing growing global cities, 2015.

Boris, as with his German invasion joke here, often repeats the same message for different audiences.

"The Dutch ride bicycles made in London, the Brazilians use mosquito repellent that is made in London. Every single chocolate Hobnob in the world is made in London!"

Speaking to the Conservative
Party Conference, 2012.

"My impression is that the vast and intricate machine of the London economy is starting to throb on the launching pad like a Saturn V rocket and as the vapour starts to jet from the valves I sense a boom in the offing."

Speaking as mayor at the third
Margaret Thatcher Lecture, held
by the Centre for Policy Studies,
London, 2013. Saturn V was the
rocket system that propelled the
NASA spacecraft for the Apollo
moon landing programme. It
operated between 1967 and 1973
and also took the USA's Skylab
space station into orbit.

TalkRadio political editor Ross Kempsell: *"What do you do to relax, what do you do to switch off?"*

Boris*: "I like to paint...um, oh, I make things. I like to. I make, I have a thing where I make* *models of. I make buses. I make models of buses. I don't make models of buses. What I do, I get old wooden crates, right? And I paint them. Suppose it's a box that's been used to contain two wine bottles, right? And it will have a dividing thing. I turn it into a bus so I put passengers - you really want to know this? I paint the passengers enjoying themselves on the wonderful bus, low carbon of the kind we brought to the streets of London, reducing CO_2, reducing nitrous oxide, reducing pollution."*

TalkRadio interview, as part of Tory leadership campaign, 2019.

Ross Kempsell became political director of the Conservative Party and was a special advisor to Boris when he was Prime Minister in 10 Downing Street. Kempsell was given a life peerage, by Boris in his 2022 resignation honours list. He became Baron Kempsell of Letchworth in 2023.

"We've begun the elimination of the bendy bus. It won't be long before the last pair of breeding bendy buses is driven from our streets."

Speaking at the annual dinner of the Federation of Small Businesses, London Branch, at the Tower Hotel, London, 2009.

Boris promised to remove bendy buses from London streets as part of his 2008 mayoral campaign. Otherwise known as articulated buses, the last examples of bendy buses were withdrawn from service in the capital city in 2011. Bendy buses could take up to 140 passengers, compared with 77 in an old-style Routemaster which they replaced. But their size meant they took up far more road space than traditional buses of either single or double decks and were blamed for blocking roads and junctions. Boris also highlighted safety issues and higher levels of fare evasion on bendy buses.

"Tube delays – which were such a big factor I seem to remember when I was trying to get elected a while back – Tube delays: down 40 per cent according to TFL. Unbelievable. And, according to TFL, average traffic speeds in our city are up from 9.3 to 9.4 miles per hour, a truly supersonic increase."

Speaking as Mayor of London at the annual London Government Dinner at Mansion House, City of London, 2014.

"I think we should give particular thanks tonight to Phyllis, the first tunnel boring machine, because Phyllis has finally expired I discovered today. Her mighty teeth have worn out, her jaws have given up: the sheer strain of chomping through the nether regions of our

67

city. And she has burrowed her way into her own tomb, they told me. And there she is to be discovered by future archaeologists. Whereas the other voracious tunnel boring machines, all mysteriously given girls' names - Delia, Nigella and so on - they're all munching towards Shenfield and Woolwich."

Speaking as Mayor of London at the annual London Government Dinner at Mansion House, City of London, 2014.

The two boring machines used on the western part of Crossrail were called Phyllis and Ada and named after artist and typographer Phyllis Pearsall who set up the Geographers' A-Z Map Company

and Ada Lovelace, a 19th century mathematician and early computer scientist who worked on Charles Babbage's proposed digital programmable computer.

"It's been an amazing day, my friends, for me - because it began as so often in my life with my finding myself this morning in a colossal hole, partly of my own making, in the sense that I was at Crossrail at the excavations at Tottenham Court Road."

Speaking as Mayor of London at the annual London Government Dinner at Mansion House, City of London, 2014.

"London Transport, TFL, pumps out billions a year to thousands of SMEs around the country, sustaining companies - very often family companies and livelihoods - by taking-in to London, sucking-in: underground escalator chains from Dudley, jumbo-lubers from Liverpool. I'll be your long-haired luber from Liverpool, as the song once went. Lift cables from Chester-le-Street, where they have the oldest cable manufacturer in the world, thought once to have been responsible for making Vince Cable himself."

Speaking in 2013 at the London School of Economics, on The Future of London Within the UK.

Little Jimmy Osmond had a Christmas Number One hit, aged nine, with Long Haired Lover from Liverpool, in 1972.

LONDON 2012 OLYMPIC GAMES

Boris launched himself full throttle at supporting the 2012 London Olympics, often in thunderous fashion. He appeared as mayor at scores of events prior to, during and after the games in a bid to build excitement, support athletes and celebrate their success: something which his early speeches demonstrate was not seen as guaranteed by many observers and commentators.

"I mourn the passing of some of these games, some of the sports [**former Olympic sports**]. *For instance the pankration, whose chief exponent was Milo of Croton; whose signature performance involved carrying an ox the length of the stadium, killing it with his bare hands and then eating it all on the same day."*

Speaking at a party in 2008, held in Beijing, to mark the handover of the Olympic flag from Beijing to London.

Pankration was an ancient Greek Olympic combat sport that used wrestling and boxing techniques. Biting and gouging were prohibited but any other tactics were allowed. The event attracted participants of legendary strength, many of whom were experienced soldiers. Milo of Croton, a six-time Olympic victor, is said to have led a Croton army to victory over the Sybarites in 511 BC.

"They have made such progress [with the building of Olympic venues] *that I have even wondered whether we should hold the Olympics a year early. It's going to be ready in 2011 – let's get it out of the way. I think there is a strong case for us in Britain to catch the rest of the world napping, call a snap Olympics and win more than one gold medal."*

Speaking as Mayor of London March at MIPIM 2010.

MIPIM is an international property developers' organisation based in Cannes, France and has an annual get together. MIPIM stands for Le Marché International des Professionnels de L'immobilier.

"The secret to that beautiful rosy hue: do you know what it is? I will tell you. That beautiful hue is achieved by rubbing it with a special substance: rhubarb. It is rubbed with rhubarb. It is lovingly rubbed with rhubarb. The whole of the exterior of this building is lovingly rubbed with rhubarb. And, therefore, this fantastic velodrome creates jobs and employment for English rhubarb growers, ladies and gentlemen. And above all it has helped create a new craft, which will go on because it will need to - because it will continue to be rubbed with rhubarb. This velodrome has created a new craft of English rhubarb rubbing."

Speaking in 2011 as Mayor of London at the opening of the London Olympics velodrome.

Oxalic acid, a compound found in rhubarb, was used but not rhubarb itself. The purpose was to seal the wood exterior of the velodrome building. A spokesman from the Olympic Delivery Authority later said: "It's not actual rhubarb or rhubarb juice."

"One thing people think is: "Why are you building these structures like this Anish Kapoor tower; this curly-wurly-pretzel-hubble-bubble

type jobby.""

Speaking as Mayor of London, asked about the cost of the Olympics, interviewed by Mumsnet, 2010.

Anish Kapoor is the sculptor who designed The ArcelorMittal Orbit sculpture and observation tower. It is in the Queen Elizabeth Olympic Park, Stratford, East London, and was commissioned to celebrate the London Olympics. Its spiral design is 376 feet high and includes a slide that visitors can chute down towards the ground on.

"We have the ArcelorMittal Orbit – the largest public art structure in the whole of Britain. You know what I'm talking about? This kind of gigantic mutant trombone jobby beckoning the world to East London like a vast mutant orchid."

Speaking at the London Policy Conference staged by the Institute for Public Policy Research, 2011.

"The ArcelorMittal Orbit - the single most baffling representation of a giant mutant trombone ever produced."

Speaking as Mayor of London at the Indian Journalists' Association UK dinner, London, 2013.

Reporter: *"How excited are you that the games are only two days away?"*

Boris: *"I'm almost incoherent with excitement. The Geiger counter of excitement is creeping towards maximum. I suppose it will really kick off on the night of the opening ceremony."*

Speaking at Middlesex University
for the arrival of the Olympic
torch, 2012.

"I've never seen anything like this in all my life. The excitement is growing so much that I think the Geiger counter of Olympo-mania is going to go zoink off the scale."

Speaking as mayor in Hyde Park,
London, at a concert to mark
the arrival of the Olympic torch,
2012.

"Our Team GB athletes are ready. They're going to win more gold, silver, bronze medals than you'd need to bail out Greece and Spain together."

Speaking as mayor in Hyde Park,
London, at a concert to mark
the arrival of the Olympic torch,
2012.

Mark Austin, ITV News: *"What keeps you awake at night? Here we are, opening ceremony* *tonight."*

Boris: *"Almost nothing keeps me awake at night."*

Mark Austin: *"Oh, come on, you're the mayor of the city about to stage the Olympics."*

Boris: *"I get up very early. I bound out of bed like a bounding, bounding tiger or something. Or a panther."*

Speaking as Mayor of London to Mark Austin of ITV News on the day prior to that evening's opening ceremony of the 2012 London Olympic Games.

"We put on the greatest Olympic and Paralympic Games ever. Did we not? And the Tube ran on time and the G4S guards all turned up and Team GB won more medals per head than any country on the planet. And the whole population was so buoyed up it was as if we had been crop-dusted with serotonin."

Speaking as Mayor of London at the Chartered Institute of Housing's 2013 Presidential Dinner, Natural History Museum.

G4S had a contract to supply thousands of security staff at the London Olympics but was forced to concede that it had not recruited enough people – just 16 days before the games began. Authorities secured 3,500 military recruits to cover the shortfall.

"Also, of course, I want to thank everybody who didn't get medals. And I speak as a Tory politician well acquainted with - you know - I know all about losing. And I know each one of you 546 who haven't yet won medals were absolutely indispensable."

Speaking as mayor to the Team GB athletes after the end of the London Olympics, 2012.

"This was your achievement. You brought this country together in a way we never expected. You routed the doubters and you scattered the gloomsters. And for the first time in living memory you caused Tube train passengers to break into spontaneous conversation with their neighbours about subjects other than their trod-on toes."

Speaking at parade of British athletes after London Olympics, 2012.

"Listen, folks, you've done the most incredible job. You've done London proud, you've done the world proud. I think the whole country looked at what you did with absolute mounting awe and stupefaction. And the question is how do we now keep it all going? How are we going to keep the momentum of the Olympics? What else do we do

now? I think we just have an orgy of... (laughter and cries of shock from audience)... no, no, no: an orgy of national congratulation and thanks."

Speaking to thank successful team GB athletes for their part in the 2012 London Olympics, Team GB House, Westfield, Olympic Park, 2012.

"The sociologists will write learned papers about that sudden feeling that gripped us all. Was it Eudaimonia, euphoria, eupepsia? Some other Greek word beginning with eu? – you name it."

Speaking to Conservative Party Conference, 2012.

Eudaimonia is a concept in Aristotelian ethics defined as the highest human good, desirable as an end in itself. Euphoria is a feeling of uttermost confidence or happiness. Eupepsia means having good digestion.

"Anthropologists will look back with awe at the change that took place in our national mood: that sudden switch from the gloom of the previous weeks. Remember, the buses were on strike. I'm afraid the taxi drivers were blockading the West End. One of them actually handed the keys of his cab to a police guy and jumped off Tower Bridge – some of the others could have done the same, frankly. Never mind. Thousands of the security staff seem

mysteriously to have found other things to do. And the weather men were predicting cataclysmic inundations for the night of the opening ceremony, remember? And then some time in that first week it was as though a giant hormonal valve had been opened in the minds of the people and the endorphins seemed to flow through the crowds and down the Tube trains like some benign contagion until everyone was suffused with a kind of Ready Brek glow of happiness."

Speaking to Conservative Party Conference, 2012.

Ready Brek is an oaty cereal or porridge. In the 1970s and 1980s it was advertised on television with images of children being accompanied by a lustrous orange glow – as if the act of eating Ready Brek helped enshrine them in a warming, rich and radiant heat.

FUTURE OF LONDON

"I predict that by the middle of this century London will have about ten, eleven million people. And it will have established itself as the unchallenged capital not just of England, not just of Britain, not just of the United Kingdom but – believe me – of Europe. And we will have by then, by 2050, we will have a population of 72 million. We will overtake Germany in the following decade – not just in numbers but probably also in economic output as well. I will go further. We will have a monarchy, we will have a union between England and Scotland and many, many things will be the same. We will have a government still trying to build a third runway at Heathrow while the rest of us have gone on to do better schemes. I predict that Mr Julian Assange will still be holed up in the Ecuadorian embassy wasting police time and resources. And the LSE, the London School of Economics, will have lengthened its lead as one of the greatest, if not the greatest higher education institutions in the world. And people will continue to come

to Britain to have a cosy tea in a Welsh pub and enjoy a traditional night out in Newcastle, as you do, or romp with a shaggy Highland cow or whatever you get up to with a Highland.... But, and this is the critical point to which I will return, in so far as that is their ambition, they will come to London first just to see the beautiful garden bridge. And that is why we need London as the world capital of finance, of culture, of law, of the arts, of live music, of tech, of fintech, of nanotech, of biotech, edtech. Tech – I mentioned tech already. But above all we will need London as the capital of Britain."

Speaking at the London School of Economics, on The Future of London Within the UK, 2013.

The various types of technology Boris refers to here are fintech – technology that supplies financial products and services; biotech – the use of living organisms to manufacture items, enhance the environment, enable better health, support the environment; edtech – technology to help people learn.

"By 2050 we will have improved the city [London] dramatically. We will have not just Crossrail, we will have Crossrail 2: linking Hackney and Chelsea. Helping all those commuters in south-west London. We'll probably have Crossrail 3, taking you out to the Margaret Thatcher International Airport in the Thames

Estuary – if not Crossrail 4. Some things, of course, will still be the same. We will still have beautiful parks and lovely pubs and the Tower of London. And Julian Assange will still be holed up in the Ecuadorian Embassy, wasting police time and resources."

Speaking as Mayor of London at the third Margaret Thatcher Lecture, held by the Centre for Policy Studies, London, 2013.

Boris was a keen backer for a new Thames Estuary Airport to be built instead of a third runway at Heathrow. Adversaries dubbed the plans for a new hub airport "Boris Island". It would have been built on an artificial island.

But the plans were rejected by the Airports Commission in 2014.

LABOUR AND
THE LEFT

Boris seems to take great joy in lobbing put-downs the way of political opponents. He name-calls, uses derogatory metaphors and makes colourful quips at the expense of his foes on the left. Ken Livingstone is a newt, Keir Starmer is Captain Hindsight. He promises to make Britain Corbyn neutral.

"It's 43.5 per cent of kids taking maths at A-level this year got an A in maths. Fantastic. If I was a Labour minister I would of course stand up before you now and, like Suslov or Khrushchev, I would hail the fantastic yields in the Donbas region and the amazing productivity of our Stakhanovite children in producing yet more grade A to C red star factories, tractors and all the rest of it. Wouldn't I? And I would say: "We must celebrate our national achievement

every year. Comrades! Our children are getting cleverer and cleverer. And their brains are sprouting out of every orifice.""

Speaking at University of Surrey Students' Union, 2007.

Mikhail Suslov was a leading Soviet politician favoured by Stalin. Nikita Khrushchev was Stalin's successor as Soviet leader. The Stakhanovites formed a Soviet cultural working movement celebrating hard work. Boris here is comparing academic grade inflation under the then Labour regime to Soviet propaganda-led industrial achievements.

"We all fought together this year to keep London from lurching back into the grip of a cabal of semi-Marxist and taxpayer-funded Châteauneuf-du-Pape swilling tax minimisers and car hating bendy bus fetishists."

Speaking to Conservative Party Conference, in Birmingham, after his success in the London mayoral election, 2012. Boris has often joked that he inherited a huge supply of Châteauneuf-du-Pape from the previous Labour mayoral regime in London under Ken Livingstone.

"It is unbelievable now to see that the Labour Party has been piratically captured in a kind of social media twitstorm by what Harold Wilson once called a small group of politically motivated men. I know these people – some of them are out there today [**protesting outside the conference hall**] *– they are the London Labour Party. Trots and militants with vested interests. And, indeed, interesting vests. They are the people who idolise Hugo Chavez and toast the revolution in taxpayer funded vintage Burgundy."*

Speaking to Conservative Party
Conference, Manchester, 2015.
Hugo Chavez was president of
Venezuela from 1999 until his
death in 2013. He visited London
in 2006 and was welcomed as
a guest by Ken Livingstone,
then mayor of the city. Chavez
described capitalism as
"destructive" on his visit.

"Surely to goodness we can take on this Tony Benn tribute act and wallop it for six. Not by imitating them, not by capering insincerely on Labour turf. We won't get anywhere by metaphorically acquiring beards or string vests or allotments but by systematically pointing out the damage they would do."

Speaking at Conservative Party

Conference, Conservative Home
fringe meeting, in Birmingham,
2018.

"We believe in free markets and enterprise and the wealth-creating sector of the economy in a way that causes a shadow of Transylvanian horror to pass over the semi-communist faces of the Opposition front bench."

Speaking in House of Commons,
Early Parliamentary General
Election Bill debate, 2019.

"That's the difference between this radical and optimistic Conservatism and a tired old Labour. Did you see them last week in Brighton? Hopelessly divided, I thought they looked. Their leader like a seriously rattled bus conductor – pushed this way and that by a... not that they have bus conductors any more, unfortunately - pushed this way and that by a Corbynista mob of sellotaped-spectacled sans-culottes. Or the skipper of a cruise liner that's been captured by Somali pirates, desperately trying to negotiate a change of course and then changing his mind."

Speaking at Conservative party
conference, Manchester, 2021.

Sans-culottes, in French, means "without breeches" and was a term applied to working class activists who took part in the radical events of the French Revolution and its aftermath during the late 18th and early 19th centuries.

KEN
LIVINGSTONE

"I was never out of the outer boroughs when I was Mayor of London, and the former Mayor of London [Ken Livingstone] *visited Havana more often than he visited Havering."*

Speaking in House of Commons, debate on Sanctions and Anti Money Laundering Bill, 2018.

ED MILIBAND

"Dawn is almost breaking. It's been a very long night. I think we should all go back to our kitchens. Go back to our kitchens and prepare for breakfast. And quite frankly I don't mind how many kitchens you have."

Victory acceptance speech on being declared winner of the election to be MP for Uxbridge and Ruislip South at the 2015 General Election, speaking on morning after the previous day's vote.

Boris's reference to kitchens is a cheeky dig at then Labour leader Ed Miliband. During the run-up to the 2015 election Miliband was pictured having a hot drink with his wife Justine in a modest looking kitchen at their home. It was soon revealed that the couple had two kitchens – with a friend saying the one pictured was only used for drinks and snacks, something denied by Miliband who said it was the family's main kitchen. He said: "The house we bought had a kitchen downstairs when we bought it. And it is not the one we use. We use the small one upstairs."

"Go back to your…" is taken from a phrase used by Liberal Party leader David Steel at the 1981 Liberal Assembly. With the Liberals and their SDP allies running high in the opinion polls, Steel said: "Go back to your constituencies and prepare for government." But the Falklands War of 1982 saw a Conservative resurgence and only 17 Liberals were elected at the 1983 general election.

JEREMY CORBYN

Jeremy Corbyn was Leader of the Opposition when Boris became Prime Minister in July 2019. Many of their exchanges took place in the shadow of Brexit, with Boris firing insults Corbyn's way that attacked his tactics and socialist beliefs. When Boris won a convincing majority at the December 2019 election Corbyn continued as Labour leader until April 2020 when he was succeeded by Keir Starmer.

"He has mentioned that he is a great eater of porridge. All I can say is that when it comes to the offer of elections, he reminds me of Goldilocks in his fastidiousness - one offer is too hot and one is too cold."

Speaking in House of Commons, Early Parliamentary General Election Bill debate, 2019.

"You, the people of this country, voted to be carbon neutral in this election. You voted to be carbon neutral by 2050. You also voted to be Corbyn neutral by Christmas by the way – and we'll do that too."

Speaking after winning 2019 election, morning after polling day, to party supporters.

"I have to say that a most extraordinary thing has just happened today. Did anybody notice? Did anybody notice the terrible metamorphosis that took place, like the final scene of Invasion of the Bodysnatchers? At last, this long-standing Eurosceptic, the right honourable gentleman, has been captured. He has been jugulated—he has been reprogrammed by his honourable friends. He has been turned now into a remainer! Of all the flip-flops that he has performed in his tergiversating career, that is the one for which I think he will pay the highest price."

Speaking in House of Commons, Priorities for Government debate, 2019.

To tergiversate is to abandon a belief or change loyalties.

"This country leads the world in satellite

technology. We're building two space ports: one in Sutherland, and one in Newquay. The whole of the UK is going to benefit from these investments. And soon we will be sending missions to the heavens of geostationary satellites. Conference, can you think of anyone who could trial the first mission? Can you think which communist cosmonaut we should coax into the cockpit? The invitation is there."

Speaking to Conservative Party
Conference, Manchester, 2019.

"I think we all have a favourite candidate for the person who is best placed to trial one of the new vessels that we propose to send into space. If it is a horizontal spaceport, I am anxious that it will take off at a horizontal trajectory, in which case, even if we were to recruit the right honourable Member for Islington North [Jeremy Corbyn] to be the first pilot, there is a risk that he would end up somewhere else on earth - maybe Venezuela would be a good destination."

Speaking in House of Commons,
PM's Questions, 2019.

"Isn't it amazing to be back here in person? The first time since so many of you worked to defy the sceptics by winning councils and communities that Conservatives had never won in before, such as Hartlepool. And, in fact, it's the first time since the general election of 2019 when we finally *sent that corduroyed communist cosmonaut into orbit where he belongs."*

Speaking at Conservative Party Conference, 2021.

KEIR STARMER

Labour leader Sir Keir Starmer succeeded Jeremy Corbyn and opposed Boris in Parliament from 2020 to 2022. He roused Boris to direct a range of insults and nicknames his way. Boris dubbed him Captain Hindsight in many debates, also moderating the affront to Captain Crasheroony Snoozefest. Boris dubbed Starmer a human bollard in other exchanges and highlighted the former Director of Public Prosecutions' perceived flip-flopping between political positions. Starmer, elected as Prime Minister in 2024, later claimed he "set a trap" that led to Boris's downfall when he asked whether all the rules had been followed during the time of the covid lockdowns and Downing Street parties.

"The right honourable and learned gentleman flip-flops from day to day. One day he is in favour

of staying in the EU; the next day he is willing to accept Brexit. The Leader of the Opposition has more flip-flops than Bournemouth beach."

Speaking in House of Commons,
PM's questions, 2020.

"Is this just Captain Hindsight leaping on a bandwagon and opposing a policy that he supported two weeks ago?"

Speaking in House of Commons,
PM's questions, 2020.

"Captain Hindsight is rising rapidly up the ranks and has become General Indecision. That is what is happening, I am afraid, to the right honourable and learned gentleman. He dithers. We get on with the job."

Speaking in House of Commons
at PM's questions, 2020.

"We have no time now to focus on Captain Hindsight and his regiment of pot-shot snipe-

shot fusiliers."

Speaking remotely (because
of covid restrictions) at
Conservative Party Conference,
2020.

"If Columbus had listened to Captain Hindsight he would be famous for having discovered Tenerife."

Speaking at 2021 Conservative
Party Conference, Manchester.

"Captain Hindsight needs to adjust his retrospectoscope, because he is completely wrong."

Speaking in House of Commons,
PM's questions, 2021.

"Any one of the eight candidates would wipe the floor with Captain Crasheroony Snoozefest. In a few weeks' time, that is exactly what they will do. They will unite around the winner and do just that."

Speaking in House of Commons,
PM's questions, 2022.

Boris was predicting that any one of the eight Conservative MPs campaigning to be his successor as party leader and Prime Minister would have what it took to deal with Keir Starmer. The victor in the contest was Liz Truss. She lasted 45 days before being forced to resign after a disastrous premiership that saw financial markets spooked and the pound fall to its lowest ever level against the dollar. Rishi Sunak, whose resignation as Chancellor of the Exchequer was a significant factor in Boris's downfall, succeeded her and reversed most of her policies. Sunak called a general election in July 2024 – losing Boris's parliamentary majority and handing Labour a huge majority at the polls.

"What does it say about the right honourable and learned gentleman that no one can name a single policy - after three years - of the Opposition: apart from putting up taxes? He is one of those pointless plastic bollards you find around a deserted roadworks on a motorway."

Speaking in House of Commons, PM's questions, 2022.

OTHER POLITICAL PARTIES

"**Jonathan Ross:** *"Do you think the Liberal Party will survive after this period, or do you think they're gone?"*

Boris: *"Well, I think, yes - that in so far as all sub-atomic particles survive - there will be some residue, yes."*

Speaking on Jonathan Ross Show, 2014.

SCOTTISH INDEPENDENCE

"What will we call ourselves if you lop off the top of Britain? Because we could no longer properly call ourselves British. We'd have to say that we were rather like the Former Yugoslav Republic of Macedonia. We were the "Rest of the UK" or something. We were R-U-K. Or perhaps we would be the Former UK. Or F-U-K. My question is what the Former UK do we think we are doing? If I could put it as delicately as that. We are stronger together."

Speaking at the London School of Economics, on The Future of London Within the UK, 2013

"That is what they say they want to do if they were to achieve independence: to submit to the whole panoply of EU law, to scrap the pound in favour of some unknown currency hitherto unbaptised - the Salmond, the Sturgeon or whatever it happens to be - and, above all,

to hand back control of Scotland's fisheries to the EU, just as they have been reclaimed by this country. What an extraordinary policy."

Speaking in House of Commons, during the G7 Summit debate/EU motion, 2019.

DEMOCRACY
AND AUTOCRACY

"Democracy produces greater prosperity, better drugs, saves lives. And anyway, who listens to the music from the autocracies? Does anybody in this audience? Nobody queues up to hear Russian technofunk music, do they? Could anybody here sing a single pop song from any of the autocracies? Which country does Taylor Swift come from? I can't remember. Look, I rest my case."

Speaking at Georgetown University Institute of Politics and Public Service, at "The Global Fight for Democracy", 2024.

.

BEING HECKLED

Demonstrator: *"Tory scum!"*

Boris: *"Leftie tossers!"*

Speaking on a visit, as Mayor of London, to Bristol where he was harangued and verbally abused by demonstrators. Boris was in Bristol to give support to Conservative candidates for mayoral and police commissioner elections, 2012.

"I came into the conference area yesterday. We had to go through a kind of Khyber Pass with protesters on either side hurling eggs and waterbombs. I drew only one conclusion from that event and that is that we need to do even more to support the wonderful Tracey Crouch [minister for sport at the time] *and to encourage more sport in schools, particularly ball games, because they managed to miss me with every single projectile that they threw."*

Speaking to Conservative Party Conference, Manchester, 2015.

POSITIVITY: ELECTIONEERING, CAMPAIGNING, OPTIMISM

A huge part of Boris's appeal to the public is his ability to promote positivity. His speeches often draw on a deep sense of optimism and an attitude that, even in difficult circumstances, things can be made better and people should look forward with hope. In interviews when the Conservative Party was doing badly at elections in the early 2000s he was keen to stress that there was still something for the party to look forward to; during the Brexit campaign he offered a hopeful vision for the UK post-withdrawal from the EU; as London mayor he championed the city's strengths and achievements. Opponents have sometimes criticised this as hyperbolic boosterism.

"If we can defeat a stale, clapped-out, miserabilist, socialist regime in City Hall and install a new administration that is so frugal that we still have not yet exhausted the old mayor's stocks of Châteauneuf-du-Pape – true! – then you, David [Cameron]*, you can defeat this unelected, unrepentant, unbelievable embarrassment of a government."*

Speaking at Conservative Party Conference, Manchester, 2009.

"Like some slumbering giant we are going to rise and ping-off the guy ropes of self-doubt and negativity."

Victory speech at event to announce the next leader of the Conservative Party, and Prime Minister, after Boris defeated Jeremy Hunt in leadership election, 2019.

"We know the mantra of the campaign that has just gone by. In case you've forgotten it – you probably have – it is deliver Brexit, unite the country and defeat Jeremy Corbyn. And that

is what we are going to do. And I know some wag has already pointed out that deliver, unite and defeat was not the perfect acronym for an election campaign, since unfortunately it spells "dud". But they forgot the final E, my friends, E for energise. And I say to all the doubters: Dude! We are going to energise the country. We are going to get Brexit done on October the 31st. We are going to take advantage of all the opportunities that it will bring in a new spirit of can-do."

Victory speech at event to announce the next leader of the Conservative Party, and Prime Minister, after Boris defeated Jeremy Hunt in leadership election, 2019.

Questioner: *"A recent opinion poll for the Sunday Times on Panelbase says that your reputation in Scotland is only slightly better than that of Jeremy Corbyn: that your personal popularity is minus 34."*

Boris: *"Minus 34: we can build on that! We can build on that, is what I say!"*

Speaking at the launch of the Scottish Conservative Party's manifesto in Fife for the 2019 election.

"On July the 19th we decided to open every single

theatre and every concert hall and nightclub in England. And we knew that some people would still be anxious. So we sent top government representatives to our sweatiest boîtes de nuit to show that anyone could dance perfectly safely. And wasn't he brilliant, my friends? Let's hear it for Jon Bon Govey. Living proof that we - you all - represent the most jiving, hip, happening and generally funkopolitan party in the world."

Speaking October Conservative Party Conference, Manchester, 2021.

Chancellor of the Duchy of Lancaster Michael Gove had been widely pictured across news media - dancing in an Aberdeen nightclub earlier in the year. Mr Gove had been drinking in a pub when he heard music upstairs and accepted the manager's invitation to visit the club where he mingled with revellers and took to the dancefloor with vigour.

PARLIAMENT

"I feel sometimes like a world class athlete with a pebble in our shoe. There is one part of the British system that seems to be on the blink. If Parliament were a laptop then the screen would be showing, I'm afraid, the pizza wheel of doom. If Parliament were a school Ofsted would be shutting it down or putting it in special measures. If Parliament were a reality TV show then the whole lot of us, I'm afraid, would have been voted out of the jungle by now. But at least we'd have had the consolation of watching the Speaker [John Bercow] *being forced to eat a kangaroo testicle."*

Speaking to Conservative Party Conference, Manchester, 2019.

St Albans Conservative MP Anne Main: *"A toxic and carcinogenic bromate plume is threatening my constituency."*

Boris: *"I thank my honourable friend for raising that point about the toxic bromate plume, which reminds me of the emanations we sometimes hear* *from parts of this House."*

Speaking in House of Commons,
PM's Questions, 2019.

"This is the first time in history that the Opposition have voted to show confidence in Her Majesty's Government."

Speaking in House of Commons,
2019, Early Parliamentary
General Election moved by Boris
Johnson as PM, which MPs voted
for by 298 ayes to 56 nos but
which did not pass because it
required a majority of two-thirds
of the whole house for it to pass.
Most Labour MPs abstained.

BRITISH FOREIGN POLICY

"Of the 193 present members of the UN we have conquered or at least invaded 171. That is 90 per cent. The only countries that seem to have escaped are places like Andorra and Vatican City."

Speaking as Mayor of London at the third Margaret Thatcher Lecture, held by the Centre for Policy Studies, 2013.

"It's been an extraordinary experience for me to be Foreign Secretary for the last few months. And together with my fantastic team of ministerial colleagues: Sir Alan Duncan for Europe and the Americas; Joyce Anelay for the Commonwealth and the UN; Tobias Ellwood for Africa and the Middle East; Alok Sharma for Asia and the Pacific, we've made literally hundreds of trips. Cats cradling the world in a truly stupefying accumulation of Air Miles: not that we can claim them, of course. No, seriously,

be in no doubt."

Speaking at Conservative Party
Conference, Manchester, 2016.

"Before the anti-pirate campaign the pirates had cost the world economy about seven billion dollars a year. When Britain stepped in the attacks stopped altogether: in fact, I'm glad to say that since 2012 there have been more Hollywood films about Somali pirates starring Tom Hanks than there have been pirate attacks. In fact there have been five films and no pirate attacks. So that's global Britain five, pirates nil."

Speaking at Conservative Party
Conference, Manchester, 2016.

Somali pirates were a major threat to international shipping in the early 2000s in waters close to Somalia. The crisis was at its peak during a period of war in Somalia from 2006 to 2009. Co-ordinated operations between countries that included the UK helped diminish pirate assaults which fell in increasing number from 2012 onwards with occasional isolated incidents still taking place in subsequent years. The aim of most pirates has been to take control of the bridge of a ship and then use a negotiator, based on land, to extract a ransom for the safe return of the ship and crew. Dozens of crew members have died either from injuries, torture or malnutrition sustained during hostage taking. Tom Hanks starred in the 2013 film Captain Phillips, about container vessel captain whose ship is commandeered by pirates.

"Every day I go to an office so vast that you could comfortably accommodate three squash courts. And so dripping with gilt bling that it looks like something out of the Kardashians. And I sit at the desk of George Nathaniel Curzon and I sometimes reflect that this very seat I occupy was once the nerve centre of an empire that was seven times the size of the Roman Empire at its greatest extent under Trajan – or was it Hadrian? I can't remember. And when I go to the map room of **Palmerston** *I can't help remembering that this country over the last two centuries has directed the invasion or conquest of 178 countries – that is most of the members of the UN. Which is obviously not a point I majored on in New York at the UN General Assembly. And I didn't. I didn't because those days are gone forever and it is a profoundly good thing that they are gone."*

Speaking at Conservative Party Conference, Manchester, 2016.

George Nathaniel Curzon was Viceroy of India from 1899 to 1905, during which time he presided over the restoration of the Taj Mahal. He was British Foreign Secretary from 1919 to 1924. Henry John Temple, Lord Palmerston, served two terms as Prime Minister. He was Foreign

Secretary from 1830 to 1841 and
again from 1846 to 1851.

"HMS Queen Elizabeth: as long as the entire
palace of Westminster!   And rather more
compelling as an argument than many of the
speeches made in the House of Commons. It has
dozens of F35s on board.   Sixty-six thousand
sausages.   And not because we want to threaten
anyone or be adversarial to anyone – either
with the F35s or indeed with the sausages. But
because we want to stick up for the rule of law
that is so vital for freedom of navigation and free
trade."

Speaking at Conservative Party
Conference, Manchester, 2021.

OTHER COUNTRIES

RUSSIA

"I have been travelling around and the other day I was at the UN General Assembly in New York. And I was talking to the foreign minister of another country. And I won't say which one, since I must preserve my reputation for diplomacy. But let's just say that they have an economy about the size of Australia, though getting smaller alas. Plenty of snow, nuclear missiles, balalaikas, oligarchs, leader who strips to the waist – you get the picture."

Speaking at Conservative Party Conference, Manchester, 2016. Boris continued:

"After a few tense exchanges my counterpart gave a sigh and said that any difficulties in our relationship were all Britain's fault. "It was you guys who imposed democracy on us in 1990," he said. And I was a bit startled by this and I said: "Hang on Sergey, aren't you in favour of democracy?" And I asked for a show of hands in the room: "All those in favour of democracy

please show." And you would have thought that this was a bit like asking Maria Von Trapp whether she was in favour of raindrops on roses and whiskers on kittens. And I'm proud to say that the entire UK side of the room raised their hands as one to show that democracy was, indeed, one of our favourite things. But much to my amazement our opposite numbers just kept their hands on the table and gave us what we diplomats call "the hairy eyeball"."

Speaking at Conservative Party Conference, Manchester, 2016.

Boris is speaking about a meeting with Sergey Lavrov, Russian foreign minister since 2004.

NEW ZEALAND

"Thank you for teaching me the hongi, which I think is a beautiful form of introduction - though it might be misinterpreted in a pub in Glasgow if you were to try it."

Speaking in New Zealand as UK Foreign Secretary after being shown the traditional Maori greeting, the hongi, in which two people press noses together while often touching foreheads, 2017.

Boris is alluding to the Glasgow Kiss – or headbutt.

ISRAEL

"I reject completely the suggestion by some corduroy-jacketed snaggle-toothed lefty academics in the UK. And by the way I've got nothing against corduroy jackets or indeed snaggle teeth – before I get totally massacred by the media. That is why I completely reject the suggestion that of all the countries in the Middle East, of all the countries in this part of the world, that this one – which is the one that is free and open and democratic – should be the subject of a boycott. I just think that is absolutely ludicrous."

Speaking at the Balfour Dinner, held by the Israel, Britain and the Commonwealth Association, 2015.

UNITED STATES OF AMERICA

"I test drive cars for one of my many ways of trying to earn a crust and it is noticeable that American cars are constructed with a huge buttock ratio. It's absolutely clear that they are designed for people who basically have to be cantilevered into the seat."

Speaking in 2006 for an interview with American TV, asked what he thought of America and Americans.

"If you think about the image of British versus American hoteliers: I think we may have Fawlty Towers but then they have Psycho. On the whole I think I'd rather be shown to my room by Basil Fawlty than Norman Bates."

Speaking as mayor at topping-

out ceremony for the Park Plaza
Westminster Bridge London
hotel, 2009.

ISSUES

ENERGY

"Thanks to British technology, there is a place in Oxfordshire that could be soon the hottest place in the solar system. It is the tokamak fusion reactor in Culham. And if you go there you'll be told that this country has a global lead in fusion research and that they are on the verge of creating commercially viable miniature fusion reactors for sale around the world – delivering virtually unlimited zero carbon power. Now I know that they have been on the verge for some time. It's a pretty spacious kind of verge. They tell me now they're really on the verge of the verge."

Speaking to Conservative Party Conference, Manchester, 2019.

Boris is making reference to the Culham Centre for Fusion Energy, based in Oxfordshire. It operates under the UK Atomic Energy Authority and is a laboratory dedicated to the UK's fusion research. Scientists from Culham visited the Soviet Union in 1969 to assess the progress of an early tokamak device. Since then Culham has centred on the tokamak reactor for most of its research. The tokamak aims to harness fusion energy to produce power. It does so by fusion of atoms which then gives energy that is subsequently kept as heat in the walls of the reactor. The concept is that such heat can then produce steam which is harnessed to give electricity using generators and turbines. A UK company, Tokamak Energy, is developing fusion for commercial use: which it hopes to make available by the 2030s. The company is a spin-off from the work carried out at Culham and is backed by investment from private investors and the UK and United States governments.

"I remember how some people used to sneer at wind power 20 years ago and say it wouldn't pull the skin off a rice pudding. Well, they forgot the history of this country. It was offshore wind that puffed the sails of Drake and Raleigh and Nelson and propelled this country to commercial greatness."

Speaking remotely (because of covid restrictions) at Conservative Party Conference, 2020.

"Lenin once said that the communist revolution was Soviet power plus the electrification of the

whole country. Well, I hesitate to quote Lenin, Tony, before the CBI, but the coming industrial revolution is green power plus the electrification of the whole country."

Speech as Prime Minister,
Confederation of British Industry
conference, 2021.

"I feel like one of those beautifully drawn illustrations of what happens in a nuclear pile when the graphite rods are taken out at the wrong moment. My blood starts to boil and steam comes out of my ears and I think I'm going to melt down."

Speech as Prime Minister,
Sizewell nuclear power plant,
2022.

CRIME, PUNISHMENT AND THE POLICE

"Anybody hazard a guess how many bikes the looters looted? The answer is absolutely correct. The answer is not three, it's not ten: it is none. I don't really know whether we should be vaguely flattered or insulted by that. But the reality is, there was virtually only one thing safer than a bike hire stand in London - and that was, of course, a bookshop."

Speaking at Conservative party conference, Manchester, 2011.

Riots that began in Tottenham, London, spread across the city and to other towns and cities in England for several days during August 2011. Disturbances began after police shot and killed Mark Duggan, aged 29, after the minicab he was a passenger in was subject to a hard stop. Protests about his death led to outbreaks of violence which

The Little Gift Book of Boris Johnson's Funniest Q...

then spiralled into riots across the country. Rioters took part in widespread looting, buildings were set on fire and bystanders were robbed and attacked. Five people were killed during the violence and more than 3,000 were arrested. Boris was on holiday when the riots erupted but cut short his trip to return to London.

Justin Wilkes of Magic Radio: *"We've just witnessed your cat-like reactions with a softball bat. I wouldn't want to be an intruder at your..."*

Boris: *"No, absolutely not. And burglary has come down very sharply in London over the last few years thanks mainly..."*

Justin Wilkes: *"To you and your bat!"*

Boris: *"Thanks mainly to the work of the Metropolitan Police Service actually, who are doing a fantastic job. But it is certainly true that I do sometimes wonder. I have a tennis racket so I think I would use a tennis racket. I wouldn't use anything more lethal than that."*

Speaking to Magic Radio the day after the opening ceremony for the Glasgow Commonwealth Games, in 2014, about his plans for the Olympic park.

"Bus crime is down about 50 per cent since I was elected. That's obviously crime committed

125

on buses rather than crime committed by buses,
which has been more or less eradicated."

Speaking as Mayor of London at
the Legatum Institute's "Vision of
Capitalism", 2015. The institute
is a think tank devoted to the
promotion of prosperity.

"Crime has been falling. And not just, by the way,
because we took the precaution of locking up the
public for much of the last 18 months."

Speaking at Conservative Party
Conference, Manchester, 2021.

Interviewer: *"Do you agree with the Home*
Secretary that the police should be a bit less
woke?"

Boris: *"Less woke?"*

Interviewer: *"That's what Priti Patel's saying:*
they should spend less time on parades, less time
taking the knee, more time policing."

Boris: *"Tell you what: I've just seen a bunch of*
police officers who woke quite a lot of drug dealers
this morning. They woke them long time before
they were expecting to have their breakfast. They
woke them with warrants. And they woke them
with the news that they were under arrest for
causing misery in the communities of London."

Speaking to Sky News after going
on police raids earlier in the day,
2022.

"I can tell you that I've just been out with the Metropolitan Police this morning on a dawn raid. Coincidentally, in Lewisham, I think maybe South Norwood. And I can tell you how important is the element of surprise. And we arrested a drug dealer, ladies and gentlemen. He was suddenly surprised to see me at the foot of his bed at five-thirty in the morning. He seemed remarkably pleased actually."

Speech as Prime Minister at Barrow-in-Furness, for the launch of the nuclear-powered submarine HMS Anson, 2022.

THE ENVIRONMENT

"I have to admit that I do not know how easily I could give up plastic for Lent. I have a plastic biro in my right hand. I propose to take it out and dispose of it in a suitable manner."

Speaking in House of Commons,
Foreign and Commonwealth
Office Topical Questions, 2018.

"This one nation Government will protect our environment with a Bill so ambitious and so vast, that there is no environmentally friendly way of printing it off."

Speaking in House of Commons,
Debate on the Address, 2019.

"We're doing this not because we are hair shirt wearing, tree hugging, mung bean munching eco freaks – though I've got nothing against any

of those categories. Mung beans are probably delicious."

Speech as Prime Minister, Climate Ambition Summit opening

remarks, 2020.

"When Kermit the frog sang It's Not Easy Being Green I want you to know he was wrong. And he was also unnecessarily rude to Miss Piggy."

Speech as Prime Minister, UN General Assembly, New York,

2021.

"Don't forget that the UK has been able to cut our own CO2 emissions by about 42% on 1990 levels and we've seen our economy grow by 73%. You can do both at once. Cake, have, eat is my message to you."

Speech as Prime Minister, Leaders Summit on Climate, virtual

gathering of world leaders, 2021.

"It's important, to go back to the original words of President Biden, it's vital for all of us to show that this is not all about some expensive politically correct green act of 'bunny hugging' or however you want to put it. Nothing wrong

with 'bunny hugging' but you know what I'm driving at."

Speech as Prime Minister, Leaders Summit on Climate, virtual gathering of world leaders, 2021.

"One of the first things I initiated three years ago was a project called Jet Zero, in which I think many of you are participating - and thank you very much for what you are doing. A zero carbon plane. And people think it's impossible. They say pigs might fly. Well let me tell you, this is not only the country that built the first jet engine but the first plane across the Atlantic. In 1909 a pilot by the name of John Theodore Cuthbert Moore-Brabazon took off with a six week old piglet in a waste paper basket tied to the strut of a Short Brothers biplane. We showed that pigs could fly a hundred years ago. And we are going to fix zero carbon aviation as well."

Speech as Prime Minister, opening Farnborough Air Show, 2022.

The basket had a notice attached which said: "I am the first pig to fly." The flight lasted for three-and-a-half miles.

SCIENCE AND TECHNOLOGY

"What does a young thrusting scientist really need? What they have and what they need and what you have provided in such glorious abundance is, of course, bathrooms. We never had ensuite bathrooms. We were lucky if you had one for the whole staircase when I was at university. But you have ensuite bathrooms in all these magnificent rooms. And I think it's very important for young scientists, of course. Not just because bathrooms have been associated with so many eureka moments from Archimedes to the invention of soap-on-a-rope. But above all you do not have to be Charles Darwin to work out that the more fragrant you are as a young scientist the more evolutionary successful you will be. And the more likely it is that by the principles of assortative mating, first propounded in this place, the genius incubated

in these buildings will be propagated down the generations."

Speaking as Mayor of London at the opening of Prince's Gardens, South Kensington, a student accommodation development by

Imperial College London, 2010.

Archimedes famously jumped out of a bath and ran naked into the streets shouting "eureka!" after he realised that measuring water displacement could determine the volume of an object with an irregular shape.

Assortative mating has been studied across species. In humans it is said to be carried out according to genetics or social and cultural factors. Genetic examples include that many males will choose a female with similar facial characteristics to their own – but the same is not demonstrated in females' choice of males. Studies show that couples are more genetically similar to each other than random people. Men and women are more likely to mate with people from a similar socio-economic group or religion, research has found.

"Where was penicillin invented? In London, but whereabouts? In Praed Street, in Paddington. And a very useful thing to have after a night out in Praed Street. Some of you who know Praed Street can testify."

Speaking as Mayor of London
at One Young World, Old
Billingsgate, 2010.

"But this technology could also be used to keep every citizen under round-the-clock surveillance. A future Alexa will pretend to take orders. But this Alexa will be watching you, clucking her tongue and stamping her foot. In the future, voice connectivity will be in every room and almost every object: your mattress will monitor your nightmares; your fridge will beep for more cheese."

Speech as Prime Minister to UN
General Assembly, New York,
2019.

"You may keep secrets from your friends, from your parents, your children, your doctor – even your personal trainer – but it takes real effort to

133

conceal your thoughts from Google."

Speech as Prime Minister to UN
General Assembly, New York,
2019.

"Good morning and welcome to this first Global Investment Summit. When you look around this museum at these strange gizmos, these proto turbines and spinning jennies, it is incredible to think that these are the winners. They are, like so many in this audience, they are the cornflakes that got to the top of the packet. Winners. I want you to think of all the millions of misshapen, mutant objects that never made it to this museum. The TVs that did not turn on. The rockets that blew up. The cars that were meant to run on rhubarb wine. Think of all those inventors in history blubbing in their scorched garages."

Speech as Prime Minister, Global
Investment Summit, Science
Museum, London, 2021.

The spinning jenny is a machine used to spin wool or cotton that was patented in 1770. It transformed the textile industry in the early Industrial Revolution, allowing thread to be spun much more quickly than previously – by using several spindles.

"The pace is now accelerating massively as companies thrust the fibre-optic vermicelli in the most hard to reach places."

> Speaking at Conservative Party
> Conference, Manchester, 2021.
>
> Vermicelli is a type of pasta –
> similar to spaghetti but often
> slightly thinner.

"1995 – an era that was technologically so primitive that people used things called car phones and went down to Blockbusters to rent VHS videos."

> Speech as Prime Minister,
> Sizewell nuclear power plant,
> 2022.

"Let's face it: it was only 120 years ago that this whole enterprise began – of heavier than air powered flight. In machines, barely more than a century ago, that looked like laundry baskets lashed together with leather and canvas and propelled by lawnmower engines. And if you can go from a laundry basket to a Typhoon in a century I just want you to imagine what the next

20 years and the next 50 years will bring."

Speech as Prime Minister,
opening Farnborough Air Show,
2022.

FOOD AND DRINK

"The other day I read in the newspaper – I think it was The Times: if you can't believe The Times what can you believe? That there was a firm in the London borough of Walthamstow that was exporting, every year, £5 million worth of brownies and chocolate cake. And where was it exporting all this chocolate cake and brownies, ladies and gentlemen? The cake from Walthamstow was going to France, ladies and gentlemen. And my message to president Sarkozy, who has designs on our financial services industry, is look to your cake industry. And my message to the people of France is let them eat cake, provided it's made in Walthamstow."

Speaking as Mayor of London to open the annual London Design Festival at City Hall, which was at that time the HQ for the Mayor and Greater London Authority, 2009.

Reporter: *"Just before you go, how much is a price of value bread?"*

Boris: *"Value bread? Well, it depends, you know – 50p? 49p?"*

Reporter: *"Ha, ha, ha – have you been genning up on your value bread? The PM [David Cameron] couldn't say. Do you buy value bread?"*

Boris: *"I can tell you the price of a bottle of champagne! How about that? Is that the kind of thing that you want me to say?"*

Speaking outside Conservative
Party Conference, Manchester,
2013.

"Food: capitalism has given us infinitely better food, I think you'll agree. Ingenious distribution centres, infinitely competitive and innovative supermarkets. I remember what the food was like in the 1970s and it was terrible, wasn't it? You could go to restaurants in London – you're all far too young and thrusting to remember the 1970s – but you could go to restaurants in London and you would be seriously offered, as a starter, half a grapefruit in a steel bowl. We have come a long, long way."

Speaking as Mayor of London at
the Legatum Institute's "Vision of
Capitalism", 2015. The institute
is a think tank devoted to the
promotion of prosperity.

"It wasn't just about rejecting Miliband and Salmond and Sturgeon and all the other fishy characters."

> Speaking to Conservative Party Conference, Manchester, 2015.

"You may have heard that curry restaurants in Britain manage to employ more people than the ship-building, coal mining and steel industries combined, which may explain the struggle that some Britons now have with their waistline."

> Speech as Foreign Secretary, Raisina Dialogue, a multilateral geopolitical conference, New Dehli, India, 2017.

"I do know that the right honourable gentleman is worried about free trade deals with America, but I can see only one chlorinated chicken in the House, and he is sitting on the Opposition front bench."

> Speaking in House of Commons, PM's Questions, 2019.

"We will take back control of our fisheries and the extraordinary marine wealth of Scotland. And it's one of the many bizarre features of the SNP

that in spite of being called names like Salmond and Sturgeon they are committed to handing back control of those fish to the EU. We want to turbo-charge the Scottish fishing sector: they would allow Brussels to charge for our turbot."

Speaking to Conservative Party Conference, Manchester, 2019.

Boris: *"A chap bet me I that I couldn't eat a mince pie in five seconds flat. What he didn't point out was that the interior of the mince pie was scalding hot."*

Stanley Johnson [Boris's father]: *"No, but you ate it. The point is you ate it while it was scalding hot."*

Boris: *"I did. I got that mince pie done."*

Speaking on Conservative Party video where Boris and his father Stanley were making a mince pie, 2019.

"Think of the potential that we have. I want a world in which we send you Marmite, you send us Vegemite. We send you Penguins and you send us, with reduced tariffs, these wonderful Arnott's Tim Tams. How long can the British people be deprived of the opportunity to have Arnott's Tim Tams at a reasonable price?"

Speaking as Prime Minister at the opening of trade talks with Australia to highlight the gains to be had from increased trade, 2020.

"It is an incredible fact that we still sell not one hamburger's worth of beef to the US, not one kebab's worth of lamb, and as I speak the people of the US are still surviving without an ounce of Scottish haggis which they continue to ban, Mr Ambassador. In fact, I don't know how they manage Burns Night."

Speech as Prime Minister, 2020, Royal Naval Hospital, Greenwich, 2020.

"From Northern Ireland: we've got Tayto Crisps. I'm a devotee. My figure is a testimonial to the benefits of Tayto Crisps. They once gave me - which I declared, of course - a big packet of Tayto Crisps."

Speaking as Prime Minister outside 10 Downing Street, 2021, to announce success of British and UK food exports.

"The Japanese have been persuaded to take more Stilton than ever before. Lucky them."

Speaking as Prime Minister outside 10 Downing Street, to announce success of British and UK food exports, 2021.

141

"Thank you for coming to this celebration of British - United Kingdom - food and drink. And it's a quite astonishing fact that British food and drink is currently sold in 207 countries around the world. Did you know that? That's what it said in my brief. That's actually more countries, I think, than there are in the United Nations. So I think we want to check that statistic."

Speaking as Prime Minister outside 10 Downing Street to announce success of British and UK food exports, 2021.

David Warburton, Conservative MP for Somerton and Frome: *"Today is National Cheese Toastie Day."*

Boris: *"Why is it only National Cheese Toastie Day? Why is it not International Cheese Toastie Day?"*

Speaking in House of Commons, October 27, 2021, PM's questions. October 27 is National Cheese Toastie Day in the United Kingdom.

Ian Blackford MP, SNP leader in Westminster: *"My goodness - I do not even think the Prime Minister can believe that tripe."*

Boris: *"The right honourable gentleman talks about tripe, and when it comes to exporting the intestines of sheep, which I know is a valuable part of Scottish tradition, even that is now being opened up around the world, thanks to the deals that this country is doing."*

Speaking in House of Commons,
PM's questions, 2021.

"We do not grow many olives in this country that I'm aware of. Why do we have a tariff of 93p per kilo on Turkish olive oil? Why do we have a tariff on bananas? This is a truly amazing and versatile country, but as far as I know we don't grow many bananas, not even in Blackpool."

Speech as Prime Minister,
Blackpool, 2022.

ART AND LITERATURE

"That was the Greek ethic: they competed for honour, for prestige, and so indeed have Londoners down the ages. Shakespeare didn't become Shakespeare by sitting alone in a garret in Stratford with a quill in his ear. He came to London and he competed to put bums on seats with Marlowe and Dekker and Fletcher and about 12 others and: pow! There was a flash and the cyclotron quivered and he became the greatest writer ever."

Speaking on Athenian Civilisation as Mayor of London to the Legatum Institute, a think tank devoted to the promotion of prosperity, 2014.

The playwrights Boris mentions are Christopher Marlowe, Thomas Dekker and John Fletcher.

"This painting above you was started in 1707, the very year when the union with Scotland was agreed – and does it not speak of supreme national self-confidence? Look at these well-fed nymphs and cupids and what have you."

Speech as Prime Minister, Royal
Naval Hospital, Greenwich, 2020.

OBESITY

"We do need as a country to address obesity and the sad fact that we are, I am afraid, considerably fatter than most other European nations apart from the Maltese, as far as I can tell. No disrespect to Malta - that is what the statistics told me."

Speaking in House of Commons,
PM's questions, 2020.

EDUCATION

"What I worry about if you have this great inflation, this great proliferation, of A-grades: that they become indistinguishable to employers. And that in itself is socially regressive. Because then an employer looks at this list of A-grades, this CV, like a man falling off a building, you know: "A-A-A-A-A." What they do then is they look to see what the school is and they go for the candidate from the good school. And that is socially regressive."

Speaking at University of Surrey
Students' Union, 2007.

"Media studies is, by the way, a fantastic degree. Listen, you snorting fellow over there! Media studies graduates go on to earn fantastic starting salaries. On average."

Speaking at University of Surrey
Students' Union, 2007.

"What it teaches me is that you can't just treat education as – what's the word? – a sausage factory. Or if it is a sausage factory you've got to make sure there are lots of different types of sausage on offer."

Speaking as Henley MP at Gillotts School, 2008.

"I am proud to say today that one in seven of the world's Kings, Queens, Presidents, Prime Ministers were educated in this country including the Japanese Emperor. We have a total global monopoly on the higher education of emperors. Thank you – it's true."

Speech as Prime Minister, UK-Africa Investment Summit, 2020.

COVID

Most of Boris's speeches during the covid crisis were by necessity devoid of jocular linguistic devices. But there are a few examples where he allowed himself to engage with the odd glimmer of creative delivery.

"I've read a lot of nonsense recently about how my own bout of covid has somehow robbed me of my mojo and of course this is self-evident dribble: the kind of seditious propaganda you would expect from people who don't want this government to succeed; who wanted to stop us delivering Brexit and all our other manifesto pledges. And I could tell you that no power on earth was and is going to do that. And I could refute these critics of my athletic abilities in any way they want: arm wrestling, leg wrestling, Cumberland wrestling, sprint-off – you name it. And yet, I have to admit, the reason I had such a nasty experience with the disease is that although I was superficially in the pink of health when I caught it, I had a very common underlying condition. My friends, I was too fat. And I've

since lost 26 pounds. And you can imagine that in bags of sugar. And I'm going to continue that diet because you've got to search for the hero inside you."

Speaking remotely because of covid restrictions at Conservative Party Conference, 2020.

Search for the Hero is a 1994 hit song by British group M People. The chorus says:

"You've got to search for the hero inside yourself,

"Search for the secrets you hide,

"Search for the hero inside yourself,

"Until you find the key to your life."

"We will ensure the next time we meet it will be face to face and cheek by jowl. And we're working for the day when life will be back to normal. Flying in a plane will be back to normal and hairdressers will no longer look as though they're handling radioactive isotopes. And when we can go and see our loved ones in care homes. And when we no longer have to greet each other by touching elbows, as in some giant national version of the birdie dance."

Speaking remotely because of covid restrictions at Conservative Party Conference, 2020.

"I know that there are some people who think that working habits have been remade by the pandemic, and that everyone will be working only on Tuesday and Wednesday and Thursday, in an acronym I won't repeat. I don't want to be dogmatic about this, but I have my doubts."

Speech as Prime Minister,
Confederation of British Industry
Conference, 2021.

FREE TRADE
AND EXPORTS

Boris backs free trade, exports and commerce. As Mayor, Foreign Secretary and then Prime Minister he used his speeches and interviews to champion British products.

"I was in Kuwait the other day and I saw this incredible shopping mall where there was a shopper buying underpants made in... Devon, which is apparently underpants city. Apparently Devon is an absolutely fantastic place to make underpants these days owing to some tax break I'd never heard of."

Speaking at the London School of Economics, on The Future of London Within the UK, 2013.

"Only the free market could produce something as ingenious as an ice cream Snickers bar."

Speaking at Conservative Party Conference, Manchester, 2016.

The first Snickers bar was created and sold in Chicago in 1930. Ice cream Snickers bars were introduced in 1989.

"I wore this morning – because it was little bit nippy when I got up – a sweater derived from a Spanish sheep, reared in New Zealand, whose wool was shorn and shipped to Italy, where it was turned into cloth that was shipped to China, then it was stitched together in China, back to New Zealand, where it was exported to France and Britain and everywhere else in the world. Think of that woolly jumper as it bounds over borders and barriers and customs posts with not a bleat of effort or exertion. That is really how trade works today with standards and supply chains that are increasingly global."

Speaking as UK Foreign Secretary at the 2017 Lowy Lecture, Sydney Town Hall, Australia.

"I met a policeman who turned out to be from Uxbridge, which I represent, who tours the world testing waterslides. Think of that: it's a tough job but someone's got to do it."

Speaking as UK Foreign Secretary at the 2017 Lowy Lecture, Sydney Town Hall, Australia.

"Our manufacturing ingenuity to my mind gets daily more boggling. I think of the factory that makes bus stops that it exports to Las Vegas. Bus stops by the way - a factory in Uxbridge. You wake up in Las Vegas, as I'm sure some of you have done, with a hangover out in the street. The chances are that you look up: there's a little piece of Uxbridge shielding you from the elements."

Speaking at Conservative Party Conference, Conservative Home fringe meeting, Birmingham, 2018.

"It is also absurd and indefensible that the population of America to the best of my

knowledge has gone for decades without eating a morsel of British lamb or beef - let alone haggis. And I have discovered that anyone wanting to sell socks to the United States - I think they at least face a tariff of up to 19 per cent. I was told that some kinds have been taken to a laboratory and set fire to twice. There are only certain ports in the United States that are licensed to receive British cauliflower. And the US military are banned from buying British tape measures as though there was still some kind of general prejudice against British rulers. So I ask you, my friends, is this really necessary?"

Speech as Prime Minister to business leaders, Hudson Yards business event, New York, USA, 2019.

SPORT

TABLE TENNIS

"Every single one, virtually every single one, of our international sports were either invented or codified by the British. And I say this respectfully to our Chinese hosts who have excelled so magnificently at ping pong. Ping pong was invented on the dining tables of England, ladies and gentlemen, in the 19th century. It was. And it was called whiff whaff. And there, I think, you have the essential difference between us and the rest of the world. Other nations: the French looked at a dining table and saw an opportunity to have dinner. We looked at a dining table and saw an opportunity to play whiff whaff. And that is why London is the sporting capital of the world. And I say to the Chinese and I say to the world: ping pong is coming home!"

Speaking at a party to mark the handover of Olympic flag from the Chinese to the British, Beijing, China, 2008.

CRICKET

"It's magical and it is very inspiring to see the flower of the British establishment, mildly inebriated, here in the distinguished pavilions in their ties and their shirts as pink as their noses."

Speaking as Mayor of London at Lord's cricket ground as England played Australia in the Ashes, 2013.

RUGBY

"It was here in London in 1871 that a group of burly, moustachioed and mildly inebriated Victorians met at a pub in Cockspur Street called the Pall Mall restaurant and decided that they had had enough of the namby-pamby pussyfooting around of the spheroid fetishists of Association Football."

Speaking in 2012 at Tate Modern, London, for the 2015 Rugby World Cup draw.

BORIS VS THE BBC

"Balliol men and women fight against injustice and low pay. Whether it's the struggle to encourage business to take up the minimum wage, the London living wage, as we have in our city. Or indeed whether it is the heroic activities of the BBC hierarchs, led by our great chancellor [Chris Patten, Chancellor of University of Oxford since 2003 and Governor of the BBC Trust in 2013] *to ensure that no hard working BBC executive should leave without a payoff of less than half-a-million-pounds of taxpayers' money. If that isn't Balliol compassion and humanitarianism I don't know what is. Well done, Chris. I congratulate you. I want you to know I advised Chris I was going to say that. He was very generous. He didn't mind. He didn't mind."*

Speaking at the 750th anniversary celebrations of Balliol College, Oxford, 2013. Boris studied at Balliol in the 1980s.

ARCHITECTURE

"Only in London could they decide to ensconce the mayor in a building which is a cross between a pile of collapsing pancakes and Darth Vader's helmet."

Speaking as Mayor of London to open the annual London Design Festival at City Hall, then the HQ for the Mayor and Greater London Authority, 2009.

"Two hundred metres from my office in City Hall there is the most withering retort to all those who say that London is in the doldrums. And the most incredible proof of the resilience of the London economy. Because you can see day-by-day, week-by-week, the adolescent growth spurts of the Shard of glass. Which will not only be the tallest building in Britain but the tallest building in Europe – do you know that? And indeed I'm thinking of moving into it just for the view of France."

Speaking as Mayor of London

at MIPIM 2010. MIPIM is an international property developers' organisation based in Cannes, France and has an annual get together. MIPIM stands for Le marché international des professionnels de l'immobilier.

The Shard, in Bermondsey, stands 1,016 feet high and is the UK's tallest building. From a distance it looks like a shard of glass jutting towards the sky. Building took place from 2009 to 2012.

"You may remember that I used to be Mayor of London. Look at the impact of the Gulf on London. The Shard – which I opened myself at least twice. The only building in the world that looks as though it is actually erupting through the skin of the planet like the tip of a super-colossal cocktail stick erupting through a gigantic pickled onion. Owned by the Qataris - as they own the Olympic village, Harrods, Chelsea Barracks."

Speech as Foreign Secretary
on the UK's policy in the Gulf,
Manama Dialogue, Bahrain, 2016.

THE CLASSICS: ANCIENT GREECE AND ROME

Boris studied Classics at Oxford University. He often includes allusions to classical figures - and metaphors from the time of ancient Greece and Rome - in his public speaking. In 2015 he shared a stage with classicist academic Mary Beard in a Greece vs Rome debate where he advocated for ancient Greece.

Sun reporter: *"In the time before you go to sleep tonight are you going to do anything to relax?"*

Boris: *"A few quadratic equations. A bit of Greek lyric poetry. Nothing complicated."*

Sun reporter: *"Do you read poetry to relax?"*

Boris*: "I do, yeah, yeah, yeah. Everybody should."*

Sun reporter: *"Not in Greek?"*

Boris: *"It's a terrible confession, but I do."*

Speaking to The Sun as part of a
day-in-the-life report of Boris on
the campaign trail for the 2019
general election.

THE EUROPEAN UNION

Boris has close ties with Europe. He spent part of his childhood living in Brussels and later worked as a reporter in the Belgian capital for The Daily Telegraph newspaper. His reports from the European Union were often punctuated with scepticism about the EU's decisions and governance – on topics as varied as prawn cocktail crisps, the power of vacuum cleaners and the curvature of bananas. Despite that, it was not until the EU referendum of 2016 that he withdrew support for the UK's membership and campaigned for Brexit.

"We are not just a valued and, by the way, fully paid-up member of the EU: which we will remain. Whether or not we are in the Fiscal Union, or FU as it's called; or whether we are relegated to the second tier of the Fiscal

Union, or FU2 as it's called; we will remain a paid-up, valued, participating member of the single market. Under no circumstances, in my view, will a British government adjust that position."

> Speaking at the London Policy Conference staged by the Institute for Public Policy Research, 2011.

"At the moment we are claiming to have capped immigration by having a 60 per cent reduction in New Zealanders when we can do nothing to stop the entire population of Transylvania – charming though many of them, almost all of them, doubtless are – from trying to pitch camp at Marble Arch."

> Speaking as Mayor of London at the third Margaret Thatcher Lecture, held by the Centre for Policy Studies, London, 2013.

"I think the people of this country have no idea of how far the EU now invades every area of our lives. And it isn't just the mindless interference telling us how powerful our vacuum cleaners can be, saying that we can't sell olive oil in carton cans of more than five litres, or bananas with abnormal curvature of *the fingers."*

Speaking at launch of Vote Leave campaign, Manchester, 2016.

"I think it was in the Daily Telegraph: if you can't believe the Telegraph what can you believe? I think it was widely publicised that the EU Commission wants to ban some British vacuum cleaners on the grounds that they are too powerful. I am perfectly prepared to concede that if you do not handle your vacuum cleaner correctly you may end up accidentally inhaling the hamster or sucking the budgerigar through the bars of the cage. And I have read that there are some people - probably the type who think of defecting to UKIP - who present themselves to A & E with barely credible injuries sustained in the course of what I can only call vacuum cleaner abuse."

Speech to Conservative Party Conference, 2014.

"When you look at the EU now it makes me think of some badly designed undergarment that has now become too tight in some places: far too tight, far too constrictive. And dangerously loose

in other places."

Speaking on a tour of the David
Nieper clothing factory in
Alfreton, Derbyshire, 2016.

"On bananas – which I've been attacked about. Indeed, they sent a person in a gorilla suit to kind of monster me. How many directives do you think there are from the European Union on bananas? There are four. Do we need them? Do we need to be told that you can't have abnormal curvature of your bananas?"

Speaking on This Morning, ITV, 2016.

"It's time we generally persuaded the Eurocrats to stop trying to tell us what to do. First they make us pay in our taxes for Greek olive groves, which probably don't exist: Potemkin olive groves. Then, I read the other day, they said we can't dip our bread in little pots of olive oil in restaurants. Here we are: we finally say we're sophisticated enough to use olive oil and they say we can't. We didn't join the Common Market, betraying the New Zealanders and their butter, in order to be told when and how we must eat olive oil that we have been forced to

subsidise."

Speaking as Mayor of London
at the third Margaret Thatcher
Lecture, held by the Centre for
Policy Studies, London, 2013.

Grigory Potemkin was a Russian
statesman favoured under
Catherine the Great in the late
18th century. The term Potemkin
Village hails from a reported
scheme that he undertook to
construct fake facades of non-
existent buildings on a visit by
Catherine to the south of Russia
and Crimea in 1787 in order
to impress her about the area's
prosperity. It is now applied to
real or allegorical ventures where
the architect of the plan wishes
to show that a state of affairs
somewhat better than the one in

existence prevails.

*"In fact we have an absurd situation in which
the EU is actually trying to veto the ivory ban
in spite of having a president called Donald
Tusk."*

Speaking at Conservative Party
Conference, Manchester, 2016.

BREXIT

The Brexit referendum debate
was transformed in February
2016 when Boris announced
he would campaign to leave the
European Union. He surprised
many – including Prime Minister
David Cameron – when he spoke
to reporters outside his home in
London, to say: "I would like to see
a new relationship based more on
trade - on co-operation - with much
less of this supranational element.
I have decided, after a huge amount
of heartache, because I did not
want to do anything: the last thing
I wanted was to go against David
Cameron or the Government. But
after a great deal of heartache I don't
think there's anything else I can
do. I will be advocating Vote Leave,
or whatever the team is called. I
understand there are many of them.
Because I want a better deal for the
people of this country. To save them
money and to take back control.
That's really I think what this is all
about."

"And I say respectfully to our stentorian friend in the blue 12-star hat: that's it! Time to put a sock in the megaphone and give everybody some peace."

Speaking after winning 2019 election, on the morning after polling day, to party supporters. Boris was giving a message to Steve Bray, a protestor who had stood outside Parliament most days during 2018 and 2019 shouting "stop Brexit" and other anti-Brexit slogans, often using a megaphone.

His chants regularly interrupted TV news reports as they were being broadcast outside the Palace of Westminster. Bray often clad himself in a cape made from an EU flag. He also sported a large blue hat. He carried on protesting after Brexit, targeting much of his ire at the ruling Conservative Government. In 2024, as Prime Minister Rishi Sunak gave his rain-soaked speech in Downing Street to announce a general election, Bray used a speaker system to blast out Things Can Only Get Better - the D:Ream song used by Labour in its 1997 campaign. Later, Bray said he had been banned from every street around Whitehall and Parliament. He said: "Apparently two people complained. Probably Rishi

Sunak and his wife."

PEOPLE

BORIS VS JEREMY PAXMAN

Boris (asked whether he would break the law regarding proposed identity cards): *"I will not obey the identity card. I have gone so far as to say that I think it tyrannical. And I will grind it up and eat it on my children's cornflakes. Or give it to my children to eat on their cornflakes."*

Paxman: *"That's generous of you."*

Speaking on a BBC Newsnight debate for London mayoral candidates hosted by Jeremy Paxman, 2008.

Identity cards were issued voluntarily between 2009 and 2010 by the then Labour Government but the act that brought them in was repealed by the coalition. Boris subsequently as prime minister brought in a host of liberty-infringing laws during the covid crisis.

Boris: *"Whatever type of wool sausage is contrived by this great experiment, the dominant ingredient has got to be Conservatism. The meat in the sausage has got to be Conservative, I would say. There will be plenty of bread and other bits and pieces."*

Jeremy Paxman: *"The question is whether it's a chipolata or a Cumberland sausage, I suppose, is it?"*

Boris: *"Enough of this gastronomic metaphor."*

Paxman: *"You started it."*

Boris: *"Well, I've had enough of it."*

Paxman: *"Haven't you got a city to run?"*

Boris: *"I have got a city to run! And that's exactly the point."*

Paxman: *"Well go and do it. Goodbye."*

Boris: *"The government of London will carry on irrespective of the temporary difficulty in providing a national government. Thank you."*

Paxman: *"Bye, bye, Boris."*

Speaking after the hung parliament of the 2010 election which led to a coalition government.

Jeremy Paxman: *"What happens after Mayor of*

London?"

Boris: *"Well, you know, that's in about two-and-a-half years' time, three years' time, and that's a long time. And as I've said before it might be that I wanted to have a career in writing romantic fiction, for instance."*

Paxman: *"It is possible. I suppose."*

Boris: *"Why not? Rosie M Banks, or some such pseudonym."*

Paxman: *"In Matthew D'Ancona's book In It Together, he quotes a conversation between you and David Cameron, where on the night of your second victory over Livingstone, you say to Cameron: "This is my last election, Dave, I want to go and earn some money.""*

Boris: *"Yeah, I mean, someone pointed that out to me earlier this evening. I mean, Matthew is a brilliant journalist and a brilliant writer. I don't remember saying that. I mean it is conceivable but I don't remember saying that."*

Paxman: *"David Cameron replies, apparently: "That's bollocks." Is it bollocks?"*

Boris Johnson: *"Um, what, the whole story?"*

Paxman: *"No, no – the idea that what you want to do when you leave the mayoralty of London is to go and make some money."*

Boris: *"I've just said, in case you weren't paying attention, that one thing I had thought of doing, perhaps in a completely vain and, er, unrealistic way, was romantic fiction. With those kind of glossy novels at airports with very embossed covers with pictures of orchids. Perhaps I'd adopt a pseudonym so that you might, you might - your hand might waver over the, the..."*

Paxman: *"Tell you what - you're not going to make a fortune out of that, Boris."*

Speaking to Jeremy Paxman on Newsnight, during Conservative Party Conference, 2013.

Rosie M Banks is character in some of PG Wodehouse's novels. She is married to Bingo Little – a friend of Bertie Wooster - and writes romance novels.

In 2014 Boris appeared with Jeremy Paxman for an item to mark the BBC journalist's final Newsnight programme. The two cycled together around the streets of London on a shaky old tandem bicycle:

Jeremy Paxman: *"This is the most stupid assignment."*

Boris: *"It's your idea!"*

Paxman: *"I've done war zones, Boris, that are easier than this."*

Boris: *"I did this as a special favour to you as I care about you so much, Jeremy. You're a landmark of our culture and I wanted to show you how delightful it is to cycle in London. This, I have to say, is the most difficult machine I have ever had to cycle-on - but Newsnight procured this."*

Paxman: *"People screaming: "There's Boris!" Does this happen all the time?"*

Boris: *"Normally people shout: "You Tory tosser!"*

Boris: *"Jesus Christ, there's the police. I'll do the talking. I'll do the talking. You leave it to me: I've been here before."*

Speaking to Newsnight Presenter Jeremy Paxman during an interview conducted as they rode a tandem bicycle together around the streets of London, 2014. The interview was broadcast as part of the last Newsnight TV show Paxman appeared on.

THE QUEEN

"Of course, there was one Olympic medal ceremony where she could claim to have bred both the rider, the Princess Royal, and the horse - a claim that will likely go unrivalled for some time to come."

Speaking in House of Commons, Address to Her Majesty: Platinum Jubilee, 2022.

NIGEL FARAGE

"As I never tire of telling my friends, we export tea to China and cake -chocolate cake - to France. We export bicycles, I am proud to say, made in London to Holland. We export TV aerials to South Korea and boomerangs to Australia, I believe. I think we have at least once in the past exported sand to Saudi Arabia. And Nigel Farage to America, I am delighted to say."

Speaking in House of Commons, debate on Budget resolutions, 2017.

"We will have those free trade deals. We already have some astonishing exports as I never tire of telling you. We export Jason Donovan CDs to North Korea, would you believe it. And we exported Nigel Farage briefly to America – though he seems to have come back."

Speaking to Conservative party conference, Manchester, 2019.

"We do extraordinary things, as I never tire of telling you. Tea to China, cake to France, TV aerials to South Korea and so on. Boomerangs to Australia, Nigel Farage to America. Then he came back of course."

Speech as Prime Minister, Royal
Naval Hospital, Greenwich, 2020.

DONALD TRUMP

"I have to say when Donald Trump says that there are parts of London that are no-go areas I think he's betraying a quite stupefying ignorance that makes him frankly unfit to hold the office of president. I would invite him to come and see the whole of London and take him round the city, except that I wouldn't want to expose Londoners to any unnecessary risk of meeting Donald Trump."

Speaking in TV news interview after Donald Trump said places in London were so radicalised that the police were in fear of their lives, 2015. Trump was elected president in 2016.

"I have to say that when I met Donald Trump he was actually extremely gracious, in spite of the remarks to which you unkindly alluded. He said, rather mystifyingly, how often he was mistaken for me. Which I thought was a low blow."

Speaking as UK Foreign Secretary at the 2017 Lowy Lecture, Sydney Town Hall, Australia.

TONY BLAIR

"The worst mistake Tony Blair... I think he's made any number of bad mistakes: the Dome, John Prescott."

Speaking at University of Surrey Students' Union, 2007, after being asked to nominate then Prime Minister Tony Blair's biggest mistake. He continued:

"I think he's made many, many mistakes. Did someone say Cherie? I won't hear a word! Do you know I don't think we should have that kind of sexism here in Surrey Students' Union. I rather like Cherie, I do. In fact I once met her on Liverpool's station. I can't remember quite what I was doing in Liverpool. Probably on my way to grovel."

Speaking at University of Surrey Students' Union, 2007.

CHRIS HUHNE

"In the immortal words of Chris Huhne to Vicky Pryce: "There are three points I want to get across to you tonight, baby." Actually, I don't know whether he said "baby". But anyway, there are three points I want to get across to you tonight."

Speaking as Mayor of London at the Chartered Institute of Housing's 2013 Presidential Dinner, Natural History Museum.

This is with reference to the then contemporary story of Lib Dem MP Chris Huhne who became the first cabinet minister since Jonathan Aitken to be jailed when he and his wife Vicky Pryce were each convicted of perverting the course of justice after she took a three point driving penalty to avoid Huhne being tipped over in to a driving ban.

THE MILITARY

"I can imagine that in the last 44 weeks there have been times when some of you may have wondered fleetingly whether it has really been worth it; when you're yo-yoing 50 feet above the tarmac on a two rope bridge with nothing to break your fall; when you're tiger crawling through malodorous slurry like the final scene of The Shawshank Redemption; when you are getting the hairdryer treatment from the RSM [regimental sergeant major] *because he has detected a blemish in the sheen of your toecaps; and he is casting doubt in front of the whole parade ground on your paternity and on the morals of your mother; and I apologise to all loving parents here, but we must be frank about the kind of thing that is said on these parade grounds."*

Speech as Prime Minister, The Sovereign's Parade, Royal Military Academy, Sandhurst, 2021.

PEPPA PIG

Peppa Pig is an animated cartoon character aimed at pre-school children. First broadcast in 2004 on Channel 5, on UK TV, the shows have now been screened in more than 180 countries. Boris was pictured visiting Peppa Pig World, in Hampshire, with his wife Carrie and son Wilfred – shortly before he gave a number of speeches extolling the benefits of the character and theme park.

"I don't know if you've heard the news my friends but yesterday I went to Peppa Pig World. Hands up who has been to Peppa Pig World? I was initially quite hesitant but I found it was very much my kind of place. It had good schools, excellent health care – there's a bear called Doctor Brown Bear, no trouble too great, always turns up for a consultation. Superb infrastructure – novel transport systems in Peppa Pig World. And safe streets, virtually no crime. But what amazed me most of all was the discovery that this hairdryer-shaped-pig has already got two theme parks in her honour in China, and two I think in America,

and she is currently exported, her shows and her merchandise, to 180 countries around the world in a multi-billion-pound franchise. Isn't that an astonishing thing?"

Speaking as Prime Minister at the Margaret Thatcher Conference Dinner, held by the Centre for Policy Studies, London, 2021.

SUCCESS AND FAILURE

"I think it's very, very important to make loads of mistakes. We don't have enough mistakes in this culture. I'm not convinced that our kids are sufficiently habituated to failure. I mean it quite sincerely. If I had to have this slogan as a piece of educational political rhetoric - this needs work – but: I think we need to bring back failure to the classroom. It needs sandpapering, and I don't want this broadcast, because I haven't cleared this with Central Office...but there's a germ of an idea in it. People have got to learn to rise on the stepping stones of their dead selves to higher things. There used to be a song by a guy called Chumbawamba, wasn't there? About how you get knocked down. Do you remember that one? And we're a bit worried about that in this country. So what we do is we keep saying to everybody: "Oh well done, darling, you did very well: have a gold star.""

Speaking at University of Surrey Students' Union, 2007.

Boris quotes here from Alfred

Lord Tennyson's In Memoriam, which says: "That men may rise on stepping-stones

"Of their dead selves to higher things."

Tennyson's poem, written in 1850, was created in memory of his friend Arthur Henry Hallam who died aged 22. It has nearly 3,000 lines of text and addresses many intellectual concerns such as evolution and religion.

The poem has yielded many now widely-quoted phrases such as:

"Tis better to have loved and lost

"Than never to have loved at all."